AF332960

Dancing in the Garden

For Mary Wertsch —
with best wishes —
William Jay Smith

Also by William Jay Smith

(A selection)

POETRY

Poems
Celebration at Dark
Poems 1947-1957
The Tin Can and Other Poems
New and Selected Poems
The Traveler's Tree: New and Selected Poems
Collected Poems: 1939-1989
The World below the Window: Poems 1937-1997
The Cherokee Lottery: A Sequence of Poems
The Girl in Glass: Love Poems
Laughing Time: Collected Nonsense
Birds and Beasts
Words by the Water

CRITICISM AND MEMOIRS

The Spectra Hoax
The Streaks of the Tulip: Selected Criticism
Army Brat: A Memoir

TRANSLATIONS

Poems of a Multimillionaire by Valery Larbaud
Selected Writings of Jules Laforgue
Collected Translations: Italian, French, Spanish, Portuguese
The Moral Tales of Jules Laforgue
(with Leif Sjöberg) *Agadir* by Artur Lundkvist
(with Leif Sjöberg) *Wild Bouquet: Nature Poems* by Harry
Martinson

DANCING IN THE GARDEN

A Bittersweet Love Affair with France

A Memoir by William Jay Smith

Bay Oak Publishers, Ltd

Dover, Delaware

Copyright © 2008 by William Jay Smith

Illustrations copyright © 2008 by Paul Rhoads

Bay Oak Publishers
34 Wimbledon Drive
Dover, Delaware 19904

All rights reserved. The use of any part of this publication, reproduced, transmitted in any form or by any means, electronic, mechanical, photocopying, recording or otherwise, or stored in a retrieval system, without prior consent of the publisher is an infringement of copyright law.

DANCING IN THE GARDEN:
A Bittersweet Love Affair with France

ISBN: 978-0-9800874-1-3

To
Sonja
with love and gratitude

One's own language is one's
mother, but the language one
adopts as a career, as a study, is
one's wife, and it is with one's
wife that one sets up home.

— Henry James
(writing to a French
student of English)

Contents

Dancing in the Garden

When you are old and gray and full of sleep,
And nodding by the fire, take down this book . . .

—— William Butler Yeats

I

Departure: the Great Dream

For many years now when I awake in the morning I recite to myself the lines of a poem. Those lines form a kind of bridge between dark and light, between sleep and waking, between the world of dream and reality. Recently the poem that has come to me is not one in English but in French. It is the famous sonnet of Ronsard's, which begins:

> Quand vous serez bien vieille, au soir, à la
> chandelle...

When I was young I thought that sonnet was the most beautiful poem ever written. There were, of course, others like Shakespeare's

> Let me not to the marriage of true minds admit
> impediments,
> Love is not love which alters when it alteration
> finds...

or Robert Herrick's

> When as in silks my Julia goes,
> Then, then methinks how sweetly flows
> That liquefaction of her clothes...

But those were poems in my own language and were my birthright, whereas Ronsard's was in another language that I had learned and hence was all the more precious and so today I savor every word of it as I say it over and over to myself. I put it down here just as Ronsard wrote it in the sixteenth century; I have simply modernized the spelling:

Quand vous serez bien vieille, au soir, à la
    chandelle,
Assise auprès du feu, dévidant et filant,
Direz, chantant mes vers, en vous émerveillant:
Ronsard me célébrait du temps que j'étais belle.

Lors vous n'aurez servante oyant telle nouvelle,
Déjà sous le labeur à demi sommeillant,
Qui au bruit de mon nom ne s'aille réveillant
Bénissant votre nom de louange immortelle.

Je serai sous la terre, et, fantôme sans os,
Par les ombres myrteux je prendrai mon repos:
Vous serez au foyer une vieille accroupie,

Regrettant mon amour et votre fier dédain.
Vivez, si m'en croyez, n'attendez à demain:
Ceuillez dès aujourd'hui les roses de la vie.

    I have known that poem by heart for over fifty years and have also over those years read any number of translations of it by English poets living and dead. Suddenly one morning I thought it strange that of all those English renditions, however successful they have been, I could not remember a single line. In my drowsy state I began to attempt myself to turn the poem into English. What I ended up with is an approximation, not a finished poem, because I have dispensed with the rhyme scheme and the splendid Petrarchan form of the sonnet. But I've tried at the same time to retain the natural conversational tone of the original and have used the same twelve-syllable line rather than the ten-syllable one that translators ordinarily adopt for the English:

When you are old one evening by candlelight,
Unwinding thread and spinning there beside the
    fire,

You'll say, enchanted by my poems you recite,
"How Ronsard sang my praise when I was
    beautiful!"

And not a single maid within your household
    then
Will not, half-drowsy from her final daily chore,
Awaken at the mention of my famous name
And that enduring glory that I brought to yours.

I shall be underground, bereft of my bare bones,
A spirit now at rest within the myrtle shade,
While you, an old bent woman, crouch beside
    the fire,

Regretting my true love that you once proudly
    scorned.
Believe me, live today, tomorrow is too late:
Come, gather while you may the roses of this
    world.

However well this may approximate what the poet is
saying, how little it captures the immediacy of the scene he
depicts and of the message it carries, which is immediacy itself.
Ronsard's words evoke in one a powerful sensuous response to
the wrinkled candlelit face of the old woman with her thin
thread, as if it were time itself passing through her bony fingers.
We hear the somber room resound to the words that Ronsard is
supposed to have written and that he is, of course, now writing.
The "boneless phantom" sends a shiver down one's spine as does
the bent and bony old woman crouching beside the fire, seeking
a bit of the warmth she might have had earlier had she accepted
the poet's love. No translation can possibly do justice to a poem
which, with the sound of every word, every note, moves forward
with an elegance akin to that of Mozart. Consider the subtle
nuances of the vowels and the breathtaking repetition of the r in

the lines:

> Par les ombres myrteux je prendrai mon repos:
> Vous serez au foyer une vieille accroupie…

That last word alone, the translation of which the dictionary gives exactly as "stooping, cowering, crouching, squatting" loses all the force of the original where the sound *is* the action.

The poem has in it all of life and death, poised as on a knife-edge one against the other, light against dark, every breath a precious moment which, if lost, can never be recovered. It is all pure feeling, compressed and conveyed in the most precise language. If viewed historically, this sonnet is just a conventional treatment of the ancient theme of *carpe diem*—seize the day—so favored by Latin poets and echoing down the centuries ever since. It is on the surface simply the expression of a poet's revenge for unrequited love, but the triumph in reality is of language itself. Nowhere in all French literature is the beauty of French more forcefully and magnificently distilled.

All my life I have felt close to France and to things French. I was born in the little town of Winnfield in central Louisiana, not far north of the Red River, along which the French had settled on what they called *la côte joyeuse*. I was disappointed to find that my family, who had come by oxcart from Georgia before the Civil War, were probably Anglo-Irish rather than French. But my paternal grandmother's maiden name was "Faith," which originally had been "La Foi," I was sure. Although I had no proof of it, I was convinced that her family had arrived with the French Huguenots in Charleston early in the 1800s.

During World War I my father had enlisted in the regular Army and had been transferred to Jefferson Barracks, just south of St. Louis on the Mississippi River, where he served as a clarinetist in the band. I was only three years old when we arrived at the Barracks, as it was always called, but I grew up there thinking that Louisiana, where my grandmother still had the family farm on the edge of a bayou not far from *la côte joyeuse*, was where I really belonged. I was pleased to discover that St. Louis was originally a French city, as its street names testified: Laclede, Chouteau, Gravois, and that the section of St. Louis County, adjacent to the Barracks, where I went to school, was named Carondolet after its founder. Carondolet had completely lost its French flavor with the arrival of the more recent German immigrants, who now occupied it almost entirely. I hated the white clean-swept steps of their houses, the neat little pots of Mother-in-law's tongue in their windows, their beer gardens, their orderly predictable responses to everything in life. The general in command of the Barracks when I was a boy had come from Prussia as a young man and had risen through the ranks of the Army. His iron hand kept the soldiers ramrod-straight, clicking their heels, and saluting at every hour of the day or night. His presence confirmed my impression that Carondolet and its surroundings had become a suffocating German enclave.

It was a descendant of the original settlers of Carondolet, Marguerite Des Loges, who still spoke the French that her parents and grandparents had spoken, who introduced me to the French language. She was the wife of Sergeant Stevens, who had the unromantic position of supervising the hog ranch on the reservation, but with it went a delightful little house in a wooded area near the ranch. Approached down a secluded winding lane, it looked for all the world like one of the ivy-covered cottages in the Doré illustrations of Perrault's fairytales and Marguerite Des Loges, as she always remained for me, rather than Mrs. Stevens, was indeed a kind of fairytale figure. When I went every afternoon after school with Hugo's thick French grammar in my hand to listen to her lift the wonderful words from its pages and put them into resonant sentences, I felt that she was leading me into an enchanted realm. The price of entry into that realm was the time spent working my way through the exercises in what seemed then a rather hefty book but it was a price I gladly paid. I worked hard and it was my sessions with her that permitted me to excel in French in high school, to win a scholarship to Washington University in St. Louis and further scholarships for graduate work that led, after World War II, to the years of college teaching, from which I have recently retired.

On this cold January evening I am sitting at the window of our New York apartment on York Avenue. It is on a corner of the twentieth floor, looking out, on the east, toward the East River and the Triborough Bridge, and on the south, out over Manhattan with the Chrysler Building and the Empire State in the distance. My wife and I have lived here for fifteen years since the building of some thirty-five floors went up, much to the displeasure of those occupants of the far more elegant Park Avenue apartments whose view of the river it now blocks. It is classified as a luxury building, but in reality it was badly built and is badly maintained. The apartments are outrageously overpriced and although supposedly "stabilized," the rents have continued to climb and have become for us, as for many other original occupants, unaffordable. With its pathetic little two-pronged fountain in a semicircle of unkempt greenery, it exudes an air of elegance, which prompted a taxi driver one day to refer to it as "Miami East." But I have come to love the place and love it even more now when I know that we are leaving it for good, as indeed we must.

The apartment is empty except for a couple of folding chairs, a bridge table, and a canvas army cot under the window next to the radiator. I have come back to the city for a few days to finish some chores and to turn over the keys to the superintendent and then to join my wife at our little house in the Berkshires, where we'll spend what are referred to rather prettily but not very optimistically as our "declining years." The bare room now resounds with every step I take and every word I utter. A friend who just telephoned said that I seemed to be speaking from inside a tomb. Perhaps it is this sepulchral emptiness that makes me appreciate all the more Ronsard's vision of himself resting in the cold earth under the myrtle leaves.

When you are old—how the words echo as I say them over to myself. And I *am* old—in a few days just after we leave here, I'll be seventy-five. I shall have lived half a century since committing Ronsard's sonnet to memory. Here I have no blazing fire to bend to like the old crone in his sonnet but only this small electric radiator.

Carpe diem—seize the day, of course. But the older I get, the more difficult that becomes, not just physically but also mentally. The only way now to seize the day, it seems, is, as with everything else, to wait until it has passed so that it may be enriched by memory. Life appears to have a circular pattern to it and with age the greater part of that circle is occupied by the past, which is lit up with varying degrees of brilliance, and the future which clearly takes up less and less of the circle, is the darker part. Dividing light and dark is the thin hairline of the present, and magnificent though it is, I cannot wait for it to move into the past, to be lit up fully so that it may endure.

Tonight I sit here crouched over the radiator with no light behind me and gaze out on a scene that will be forever etched in my memory and that I shall carry with me to the grave. The apartment building directly in front blocks my view of the river but between it and Doctor's Hospital to my right I can see the tip of Gracie Mansion, the Mayor's residence, and the dark foliage of Roosevelt Island. To the left on the edge of another apartment I have a full view of Hell's Gate, the narrow, once perilous, passage on the rocks of which ships in the past had foundered. It was here that the most deadly peacetime maritime disaster in United States history occurred when in June 1904, the steamboat *General Slocum* burned and sank with the loss of over a thousand lives. The currents are still treacherous but the river, on this cold night with its full moon as it opens out toward the Triborough Bridge, is a broad black looking glass held up by the double strands of green lights that trail from the towers of the bridge and edge the lights of cars moving along on the opposite bank. From time to time a blood-red streak of light blinking in the distance cuts across its fish-scaled surface and the light on a circling plane against the black sky shimmers like the brush stroke in a Monet painting.

I have turned away from the scene several times, wanting to fix it forever in my mind, but when I turn back and gaze down, the lines of Ronsard's poem keep running through my head and I see mirrored below me in the black water the familiar face of a beautiful young woman and then with the flickering of light that face changes into the brooding face of the wrinkled old woman she has become and then, as I gaze further, beside the young woman's face is that of a young man and with a further flickering it too has changed into the lined bent face of an old man. The face of the young woman is one I have not seen in more than fifty years and the face of the young man is mine. I close my eyes and when I open them again, I see the young pair in an amorous embrace caught as on a medallion on the moonlit water. I see clearly now why Ronsard's lines have been returning to haunt me regularly: inextricably linked to their every syllable like vine leaves circling a marble slab are the threads of a story that I have to tell.

It begins when at the age of twenty I set off to study in France for three months at the Institut de Touraine in Tours. On an afternoon in early June 1938, I sat in New York in my cabin on the SS *Champlain* of the French line and reviewed in my mind all that had brought me to this point of departure into what I felt was a great dream that would change the course of my life.

Preparation for that departure had begun when as a freshman at the university in St. Louis I had enrolled in an intermediate course in French, one I had selected because the catalogue told me that it was taught by a Frenchman, M. Albert Salvan. We began the course by reading excerpts from *Le Grand Meaulnes* (The Wanderer) a novel by Alain-Fournier that had appeared not long before. I was enchanted by the scene in which the tall adolescent Meaulnes seems to be moving in and out of a dream. As one of our first assignments we were asked to write a short composition and were given a number of topics from which to choose. "Silence" was the one I chose. I had put aside my homework and had walked with friends through the woods of the Barracks to a movie. On the way home our quiet steps over the leaves and fallen twigs broken only by the occasional hooting of owls and our eyes fixed on the vast star-filled sky above us, I thought of what Pascal had said: "The eternal silence of those infinite spaces frightens me." And I thought how the French explorers cutting through the dark water of the Mississippi for the first time in their canoes must have felt at the center of that great silence. In a kind of passionate surge I put all this down, summoning up all the French words I could find and went to bed thoroughly unhappy with my effort. Two days later in class when M. Salvan returned our corrected papers, he kept mine in his hand and when I thought he was about to embarrass me because of my many errors, he read it from beginning to end to the class and said that it was a publishable essay and astonishing to be the work of a young American. He asked me to go with him to see the head of the French Department who immediately advised me to drop the education courses that I was taking and to enroll in advanced literature courses in French and to major in French since I clearly had such a good start in that language. Of course I took his advice, and soon, as a result of it, in a seminar on Marcel Proust that I had been allowed to audit, I met Stuart Chambers, who became my mentor and my closest friend. Stuart, five years older than I, was a senior not only fluent in French and conversant with the best French writers but also a poet who had published award-winning verse in a number of little magazines. Well over six feet, he seemed even taller because he walked with a buoyancy that made him appear ready to leap forward at any moment to meet any new challenge that life might offer. He was not handsome but had ordinary delicate but unremarkable features, a pencil-thin nose and mouth, both set in a fair-skinned face that flushed easily. It was his eyes that were extraordinary, a dull gray-blue that lit up like the underside of a crashing wave when, with a resonate voice and quick bubbling laugh, he gave vent to an unending irrepressible enthusiasm on every subject he attacked.

There were several of us who gathered around him following intently every pronouncement he made on literature. He introduced us to Laforgue and Apollinaire and held forth at length on *The Wasteland* of T. S. Eliot and the *Ulysses* of James Joyce. Although at the time I understood very little about either one, I was sure that with Stuart's assistance one day I would.

Stuart classified everyone he met according to whether or not he or she had a soul.

"He has no *soul*, that guy," he would say emphatically about some blunt insensitive type.

I had never heard anyone outside of church speak of people's souls, but I soon felt as he did that this was the most important of human attributes. Whatever else I had, having been admitted to Stuart's little circle, I knew that I had a soul and that alone set me apart from my dull classmates.

Every young woman Stuart met was immediately under his charm and he was the envy of all the other young men who were studying literature or striving to create it. I stayed with him frequently at his house near the university and in one corner of the sun porch where I slept he had installed an archive of photographs of his conquests past and present. He spoke as if taking these beautiful creatures off to bed had been the easiest and most natural thing in the world. Seize the day indeed he did, and he had a mistress, as all young men, or at least all young Frenchmen that I had read about, were intended to have. He wrote poems and stories dedicated to the latest of these and set down in black ink on long legal pads in such careful script that it looked as if they had already been published.

A year after we met Stuart left on a fellowship to spend two years at the Sorbonne in Paris. As soon as he left, we all waited anxiously for his letters that detailed in that careful black script his adventures, and, as I gathered reading between the lines, his continuing conquests. No one waited more eagerly for those letters than his current love, Franny Millwood, a tall dark-haired willowy creature who looked, wherever she happened to be, as if she had just risen, naked and fine-boned, from a *déjeuner sur l'herbe.* She always had one or more of Stuart's letters in her hand when she joined us for lunch at the Art School Cafeteria, the walls of which were covered by the latest awkward and rather oppressive nude studies executed by current art students. Franny would read us long segments of the letters, looking distractedly from time to time at her wristwatch, which she kept on Paris time so that she would know exactly what Stuart was doing at every hour of the day or night. I wasn't at all certain that he was precisely where she pictured him to be. In any case, I was delighted to think of him there, enjoying all the sensuous pleasures that Paris had to offer, and I was determined to make every effort to join him as soon as possible.

I had been unable to convince the committee that handled my scholarship to send me for a junior year abroad and without their help I didn't see how it would be possible to get to France otherwise. But then a classmate in one of my literature courses who had just returned from such a junior year described to me in detail the first summer months of the program spent in perfecting his French at the Institut de Touraine in Tours. This institute, in a part of France that prided itself on speaking the purest French, offered special courses for foreigners during the summer. I wrote to the Institut and decided at once to see if I couldn't manage somehow to get there on my own the following year. With that thought in mind I accepted a summer job as chauffeur and babysitter for a rich family on the shores of Lake Michigan, saving every cent I made, and during the fall semester in St. Louis worked part-time as a waiter. No one in my immediate family had ever attended college, much less studied abroad, but my mother, convinced that this trip would be important for my future, managed to borrow the final $500 that I needed.

Since I was to travel by bus to New York, my parents decided that I could for a few dollars more travel first to see my eighty-three-year-old grandmother on the family farm in Louisiana and continue across the southern states to New York. And so I did in a long journey that took me back to the Louisiana of my early boyhood and opened up to me a part of the country that my ancestors had known but that was wholly new to me. As I sat in my cabin on the SS *Champlain* I went over it all—my grandmother there in her rocking-chair on the porch of the house in which I was born, the sight of an armadillo digging below the steps, the taste of the cornbread, fried okra, biscuits and gravy that Grandma served up to me, the holly tree beside her in the yard, the bearded oaks, the pine forests and the red hills that I crossed, the musical voices and laughter of the blacks who filled the bus in Alabama whom I, the only white passenger, would willingly have sat among had the driver not summoned me to join him up front. On the final segment of the trip from Washington to New York, I met a fellow student who was also visiting the city for the first time. We decided once we had put down our bags in the YMCA where we were both staying to explore the city together. We wanted first to see Greenwich Village, about which we had heard so much. But we managed somehow to lose ourselves rather quickly on the subway, and when we finally emerged and entered a bar, we asked the bartender to direct us to Greenwich Village.

"You're right in the middle of it," he said.

We finished our beer and returned to the YMCA disillusioned that New York on this short inspection had failed to yield few of its secrets. But the SS *Champlain*, on which I embarked the next afternoon, was an immediate and thorough delight. My third-class cabin with its four bunks was far from luxurious, but the attention of the stewards made it so. And hearing everywhere around me the wonderful language that I had waited years to hear was thrilling. When the SS *Champlain* sailed, I was, for all practical purposes, already in France, and the central focus of life on board, as it is in the country to which the ship was headed, was the dining room. The newly appointed tables with their crisp white linen seemed to me straight out of an Impressionist painting, and I had been fortunate indeed in the dinner companions that had been selected to occupy mine with me. Presiding over it with immediate graceful but firm authority was Jacqueline Dumont, the wife of a horn player in the Boston Symphony. Alert, warm, and witty, her black hair always immaculately in place and her black eyes flashing, she was that proverbial French woman of a certain age who effortlessly exuded charm. She dressed with the greatest simplicity, but one knew that the scarf thrown in the seemingly most insouciant way had been arranged with the greatest care, as had everything about her person. Her presence was regal and commanding and her dinner companions placed themselves immediately and willingly at her service. Opposite her sat Janet Cleveland, in sharp contrast to Mme Dumont, plain but pretty, although in a rather severe way. Her near absence of make-up seemed to say that she was willing to let her face speak for itself but she was certainly not going to help it along. Her dress, like her entire person, was tasteful but direct, purposeful, and pleasant. She was a doctoral candidate at Cornell and her field was the seventeenth century. Her father, who had been the head of the French department at Brown, had a considerable reputation in that field. He had died just a few years before and she had set out to follow in his footsteps and do justice to his memory. With him she had spent long periods in France, had been in school in Paris as a child, and spoke impeccable French. The fourth person at the table did not need to state his professional calling; it was written all over him—in his looks, his manner, his speech, and in his trim black moustache as well as in the careful part in his slick black hair. He was pompous and slightly prissy, measured in his delivery and given to making long explanations where none were really called for. Professor Alberto Trova, who taught French and Italian at Oberlin College in Ohio, was on one of his regular summer excursions to France. He was the author of a best-selling French grammar, to which he lost no time in calling attention.

The conversation began with what appeared to me a thunderbolt, and it went on whizzing, streaking, past me like lightning from every side.

"*J'ai été sidérée!*" Jacqueline Dumont exclaimed.

I have forgotten what it was that she was thunderstruck,

flabbergasted, or staggered about. My dictionary told me that the adjective *sidérée* had originally meant "struck dead by lightning or apoplexy," and in her constant use of it that appeared to be the force Mme Dumont gave it. If she was constantly *sidérée*, I was equally staggered by whatever it was she was staggered about and went back to my cabin, where I lay down in my upper bunk dizzy from it all.

If I was dazzled and somewhat confused by the first evening's dinner conversation, I was put completely at ease by that of the following evening. The subject of poetry came up, and Jacqueline Dumont immediately declared that her favorite poem was Ronsard's sonnet:

> Quand vous serez bien vieille, au soir, à la
> chandelle...

And without any prompting, we were soon all four reciting it from memory. I was thrilled, and felt that with these beautiful lines of Ronsard's, I had indeed in a sense seized the day and that everything would be smooth sailing from then on.

The four of us were constantly together—at the table, on the deck, and in the evening at the movies. While Professor Trova paid court, if one can so designate his pompous fussing, to Janet Cleveland, I was always at the side of Jacqueline Dumont, adjusting the blankets on her deck chair, running errands for her. Responding to her every wish that was conveyed in her clear, beautiful, distinct French gave me a feeling of exhilaration. I was ready to do whatever she asked.

I had brought with me a copy of Ronsard's poems. She immediately took it up and began to read the poems aloud, explaining and commenting as she went along. I was completely under her spell as she read out:

> Mignonne, allons voir si la rose
> Que ce matin avait déclose
> Sa robe de pourpre au soleil....

And I was right there with Ronsard and his darling watching with delight the roses opening before their enchanted eyes.

The voyage went by so quickly and so pleasantly that I couldn't believe finally that I was holding in my hand the handsome printed menu for the *Dîner d'adieu*. Although as the menu put it, we were still *en mer*, it was clear that our crossing would soon come to an end. I loved every bit of that final dinner from the melon "*frappé au porto*" to the "*turbotin poché sauce mousseline*" to the "*poularde en cocotte fermière*" to its conclusion of "*biscuit glace 'Champlain'*," "*Frivolités*," and "*Corbeille de Fruits*."

When the dinner was over I asked each of my companions to sign that menu—so that their names would be fixed indelibly in my memory along with the taste of that delicious dinner. We lifted our glasses in a series of toasts and went off to bed in high spirits, our circle of friendship to be broken the next day, but I trusted not forever, by our disembarking at Le Havre and boarding the boat train for Paris.

In the confusion of disembarking I was again at the side of Jacqueline Dumont. In a state of extreme agitation, she surveyed the scene of what the French term a *bousculade*. Everyone was rushing hither and thither, back and forth, up and down the gangplank, calling to one another, struggling to get help to put the luggage on to the train. Mme Dumont thrust some money into my hand and told me to find a porter at once to deal with our luggage before they were all engaged. I managed to find one and went with him to see that everything was carefully in place on the train. I returned to tell Jacqueline Dumont that the mission had been accomplished. She still appeared nervous and it struck me that she would be clearly unhappy with whatever I had to say even before she heard what it was.

"How much did you tip the porter?" she asked. I hesitated and then told her. Whatever I had given him—and it didn't seem to me an exorbitant amount—it was twice what he should have had.

Jacqueline Dumont was at once transformed, from the classic statuesque beauty that I had known during the entire crossing, into what seemed a raging beast. Her eyeballs swelled out, the lines on her cheeks hardened down to the corners of her mouth, from which poured a torrent of invective. She called me an absolute ass, a simpleton, an idiot, a good-for-nothing imbecile. With her dark curls shaking and her whole face moving towards me with a kind of crazy snarl, she looked for all the world like an enraged black poodle that was being held in check only by the gold chain around her throat. She finally calmed down long enough to tell me to go back immediately, find the porter, and ask for half of what I had given back. There was nothing to do but obey her and I set out again. When I found the porter and revealed the reason for my having sought him out a second time, he said that the money had gone into the pool with the other tips and that there was no way that he could possibly retrieve it.

Even more enraged by the failure of my second mission, Jacqueline Dumont let loose a further stream of invective. Even though I could ill afford it, I offered to reimburse her for the money that I had foolishly parted with, but that offer threw her into an even greater rage. She let me understand that it was not the money that mattered, it was the principle involved. She quieted down, turned away, and did not address another word to me during the entire train journey.

As I stared out at the trim fields and the harmonious little villages through which we passed, the dream into which I was traveling literally revealed itself minute by minute as from a Chinese scroll. As dark came slowly down and the lights went on in the villages, I realized that however harmonious and beautiful the scene at first appeared, my great dream would clearly have its rough moments.

II

The City of Light

Stuart Chambers had written to say that he would meet the boat train and take me to a room he had rented for me near him in the Latin Quarter. When the train pulled into the Gare du Nord, I thought that I would have no difficulty spotting his tall frame and bright red face. But I looked in vain up and down the platform; he was nowhere to be seen. I found another familiar reddish face that rested on less imposing shoulders. It was that of Dr. May, a rotund pleasant old gentleman who had taught Spanish for years at the university in St. Louis and had recently retired. He explained that Stuart was unfortunately busy that evening and that he would take me to my room.

Dr. May looked for all the world like one of those self-portraits of Edward Lear, his great spherical mid-section protruding and seeming to pull him forward as he ambled through the crowd, a little fedora perched on his head. His tiny birdlike eyes, enclosed in wire-framed glasses, darted constantly about as he spoke. And he spoke steadily. He had spent many years in the diplomatic corps and appeared to know every language that anyone could mention. But he spoke them all with the same dry Texan intonation of his youth. He had a fund of stories about every place where he had been stationed around the world and never stopped telling them.

If at other times Dr. May, although a dear, was something of a bore, that evening he seemed to be a figure akin to those plump pashas in the Arabian Nights seated on a magic carpet, as he led me across Paris in our taxi. The whole city opened up before us like a great plant of green and gold with the crowds in cane-backed chairs at brass-rimmed tables on the café terraces along the avenues, their bright faces and their cigarettes reflected in the mirrors behind them, lakes of light held in their dark mahogany frames, shining bulbs in golden brackets rising along their rims. The fiery light seemed to dance from building to building, and the black intricate patterns of the grillwork on the balconies were a kind of calligraphy that hinted at delightful secrets held behind their white-curtained windows. The fire leapt from mirror to mirror, and I had the impression of being welcomed to the city with rows of torches held up in celebration of my coming. The fire outside was soon blazing in me, and I went to bed that night in my little room in the rue du Sommerard behind the Musée de Cluny warm and incredibly happy.

The next morning after coffee and croissants at the corner café, which offered up all the wonderful aromas that I had always associated with Paris, I joined Stuart on his little balcony overlooking the place du Maréchal Berthelot in front of the Collège de France. We sat in the sunlight surrounded by an assortment of books. Stuart, his old expansive self, was soon regaling me with an account of his adventures of the previous night. He had got back late and had no sooner started to doze off when he was awakened by the sounds of the violent love-making of the couple in the next room.

I gazed down below us on the little square at the bust of Ronsard that had caught my eye on arriving. Set in a small gravel circle on a green sward, the poet's long nose and tipped beard pointed down to the rue des Écoles, the two tips of a laurel wreath meeting at the top of his forehead. The bust was inscribed to Ronsard and French poetry, and below it carved in relief, two on each side, were the names of the other six members of la Pléiade, which had dominated French poetry during the Renaissance.

As Stuart continued his graphic description of his next-door lovers, I had my eyes fixed on Ronsard, whose message to seize the day–and the night– seemed oddly apropos.

Dr. May soon appeared and we left Stuart to his studies or whatever other activities consumed his time. Dr. May turned all of Paris into a classroom and for the next two days I was his attentive, enthralled, student. He explained right off that we were in what was called the Latin Quarter because the teaching here and all official exchanges between masters and students, had been in Latin until the Revolution in 1789. The priest Robert of Sorbon (Sorbon was his native village in the Ardennes), the confessor of the king, Saint Louis, here founded in 1257 a college (now the Sorbonne) where sixteen poor theology students were sheltered and taught. This became the center of pre-Revolutionary theological study and the seat of the University of Paris. It was in this same building in 1469 that three printers, summoned from Mainz by Louis XI, established the first printing press in Paris. Now the whole area overflowed with books. From one bookstore after another books poured out onto the streets, books in every language and on every subject, scholarly books, artists' books, dictionaries, geographies, histories, every aspect of the world bound up in covers and awaiting avid delighted readers. The stalls along the Seine opened out like upended trunks spilling their treasures—maps, engravings, portraits, pamphlets, postcards—onto the wide-eyed dazzled public of which I was happily one.

Dr. May took us all over the Latin Quarter, into the Panthéon, through the great vaulted interior of Notre Dame with its incomparable rosettes of stained glass, along the Seine, and finally down under the Art Nouveau sinuous iron flowers of Hector Guimard framing the entrance of the Paris Métro, up to the broad Champs Elysées, along the rue de Rivoli, and finally past the Winged Victory of Samothrace on the stairs of the Louvre announcing the treasures housed above it. Dr. May's pronounced rotund frame easily made way for us through the crowds in the immense galleries, their arches opening on infinite horizons, until at last we stood, with hundreds of others, before la Jaconde, the Mona Lisa of Leonardo da Vinci, as if her enigmatic smile were the key to all Parisian mysteries.

After a simple lunch of *poulet* and *pommes frites*, Dr. May took me back to the Sorbonne where we had started and left me in front of a statue of Montaigne at the base of which was the inscription: "Paris has held my heart since I was a child. I can claim to be French only because of this great city, great in its incomparable variety, the glory of France and one of the world's noblest ornaments."

This introduction to Paris had left me surfeited and limp, enchanted but drained, elevated to incredible heights but at the same time somehow wounded psychically and physically. Paris had won my heart completely as it had that of young Montaigne. But I was like a child returning from a first visit to a circus, all the bright colors, the sounds, the smells, the arcs of the aerialists cutting through the air, the faces of the clowns smudged and smeared, leaping forward—the whole sensuous experience so overwhelming that his body cannot cope with the psychic intoxication and as a result he takes to bed with a fever.

Stuart invited me to lunch the next day in a tiny restaurant on the second floor of a building at an angle of the boulevard St-Michel and the rue Racine opposite the Gibert bookstore.

The restaurant was packed with students and the waiters made their way with difficulty around the crowded tables.

Stuart asked me how things were going.

"Very nicely," I said. "Dr. May was so thorough in his tour yesterday that he covered several centuries in a few hours. And there is still so much more to see."

"Of course there is. Why don't you stay here longer instead of going off to Tours, where nothing is happening?"

I found his question offensive. As he asked it he seemed to rise up in his chair as if he were looking down on me from a great height. I began to wonder what it was that I had so admired in him. In his arrogant self-assurance he ignored completely the struggle that I had had to follow this far in his footsteps.

"Maybe nothing much is happening there but it's the only place I can afford to go for the entire summer," I said. "In fact I can only afford one more day in Paris."

Stuart told me how sorry he was that he would be tied up and unable to show me around any further on that last day.

"Dr. May will take you wherever you want to go I'm sure." He rose up, shook my hand, and wished me well.

As I watched him weave briskly through the crowd, I could see he did not think that my summer would add up to much.

I walked up the boulevard St-Michel to the Luxembourg Gardens where I sat for an hour on a bench watching a great variety of Parisians young and old stroll past, all emanating a carefree spirit and a triumphant joy that nothing however terrible it seemed could ever dispel. Above, the great green leaves of the chestnut trees beckoned them on as if to a celebration. I put aside any thought of Stuart's chilly reception and went back, warm and happy, to the rue du Sommerand to rest.

Because I had grown up on an Army post Dr. May took me on my final morning to the Invalides to visit the Museum of the Army and Napoleon's tomb. We went first to the Eglise du Dôme (the Dome Church) which Louis XIV had commissioned Jules Hardouin-Mansard to build in celebration of the Sun King's glorious reign. Its gilded dome, a superb example of the proportion and balance of the Grand Siècle, is now one of the unforgettable landmarks of Paris. After a brief visit to the museum we ended up gazing down in the crypt on the majestic red porphyry sarcophagus of Napoleon resting on its base of green granite, encircled by the twelve colossal statues by Pradier representing all the Emperor's campaigns from the Italian victories of 1797 to the defeat at Waterloo in 1815.

Dr. May told me then the story of the return of Napoleon's body to its resting place here. After long years of negotiation, the British finally allowed King Louis Philippe to send his son, the Prince of Joinville, in 1840 to the island of St. Helena to collect the Emperor's remains. After a long sea voyage the body was disembarked at Le Havre and brought up the Seine to Paris. A state funeral was held on 15 December 1840. Just as the hearse passed through the Arc de Triomphe and down the Champs Elysées, a violent snowstorm swept over the city, a powerful ironic reminder of the snow that had followed Napoleon back from Russia.

Dr. May's energy was inexhaustible and back in the Latin Quarter he proposed to take us immediately through the Musée de Cluny. As much as I wanted to explore the treasures of the Middle Ages that it contained, I begged off. Late that afternoon I sat again on the Boul' Miche and all the signs, sounds, and smells of the city like the drapery on the Winged Victory came swirling around me, the blue haze of the Gauloises, unlike any cigarette smoke I had ever encountered, permeated everything. And all the tables on the café terrace seemed to be edging toward me, the faces above them smack up against one another, seen as Picasso appeared to see them, from all angles at once. The Arab vendors moving among the tables, carpets slung across their shoulders, gave the boulevard the look of a souk and color was everywhere, oozing, raw and wild, as on to a painter's palette. Of the smells emanating from all sides, the strongest came from the *pissotière* on the curb just a few feet away. Like many others I had found it a great convenience to be able to step within the iron screen to a public urinal. But once inside the urine so permeated not only the ground encircling the area but the screen itself that appeared to have been rusted away and prominently displayed the holes the urine had eaten into it. So when I left, the memory of the place stayed with me and as I watched the others who followed me out, I pictured them, the way Picasso might have in a painting, each buttoning up his fly with one hand while with the other he gripped a rusty disintegrating panel of the *pissotière*. The richest colors, for which I was totally unprepared, were those of women's hair— every tinge of red and gold. The most prevalent shade was a kind of nasturtium orange-red which, in crinkling curls around their rouged faces, smoldered like red hot coals. Among the women I had grown up with, dyed hair was frowned upon. The heavily hennaed hair and thin high heels of a sergeant's plump wife had been the talk of the Army post I had known as a boy.

The blue Gauloise haze, accented by the nasturtium orange-red of the ladies' hair, was broken suddenly by two square familiar American faces that I recognized at once. They were those of Dick Gifford and Walter Williams, both students at the University of Illinois, who had crossed with me on the *Champlain*. They were bubbling over with excitement as they pulled up chairs to my table. They told me about everything they had seen in Paris, and about the best that was yet to come. They were going that night to visit Le Sphinx.

"You haven't heard of Le Sphinx?" they asked.

"No," I said, "What is it?"

It was, they explained, the newest of the famous Parisian brothels. They made it clear that they planned to go not as customers but just to have a look, and invited me to join them.

"There's a bar," Walter said, "where we can have a beer and stand and watch."

Then they launched into all they knew about the bordello scene in Paris. One of the best known was called, in English, One Two Three. Another, Le Chabanais, was right next to the Bibliothèque Nationale and was, according to some, along with the Louvre and the Eiffel Tower, one of the principal historic monuments of Paris. Beside its richly decorated Hindu and Chinese rooms, it had a special one that contained a red copper bath tub that Edward VII, one of the clients, used to fill with champagne.

That evening Dick and Walter came to pick me up. We took the Métro to the Gare Montparnasse and from there walked over the few blocks to the boulevard Edgar Quinet, opposite the Montparnasse cemetery. Here, at Number 31, two stone sphinxes guarded the entrance to Le Sphinx.

My only previous visit to a brothel had been in downtown St. Louis, where not far from the waterfront, I went with several of my comrades to a street where black women, naked to the waist, leaned from the open windows over their cans of beer to beckon us in. We went in to watch one of them spread her legs on a bed as we gathered round while with cries of ecstasy and amusement she slowly twisted a Coca-Cola bottle deeper and deeper into her vagina.

That hot dark riverfront St. Louis room was in sharp contrast to the Parisian one that confronted me now. If the original sphinx had been slow to disclose its mysteries, this one seemed eager to reveal everything at once. On a huge dance floor, the walls of which were paneled in dazzling gold, an immense gold sphinx stared from the center wall. Over the bar to the right where we went to stand were gold-draped Egyptian figures in long robes, their hands demurely at their sides.

Before this golden backdrop swirled the ladies of the night, in high spiked heels, completely nude except for a small *cache-sexe*, from which hung a long strip of gauze like a mysterious floating handkerchief. Their hair had all the colors that I had contemplated on the café terrace that afternoon, with a predominance of the nasturtium orange-red that matched perfectly the orange nipples of the breasts of all shapes and sizes that shook as, laughing and joking, they danced with their fully-clad prospective customers who also came in all shapes and sizes.

While the high heels clicked and clacked on the glossy floor, gauze garlands whirled as the ladies spun round and round before us to the strains of a popular song belted out by a little jazz trio in the corner:

> Parlez-moi d'amour
> Redites-moi des choses tendres
> Votre beau discours
> Mon coeur n'est pas las
> De l'entendre.
>
> Speak to me of love
> Say those sweet things again
> My heart will never tire
> Of hearing your lovely words.

As I watched this panorama of pink flesh floating by against the gold background to this sweet music, I had the impression that all the nudes I had seen in the Louvre had been wrenched from their frames and were drifting before me, the strands of the drapery they had been holding now torn off and dangling in shreds from their lovely bodies.

The saxophone reached its climax as we turned to go:

> Rien n'est plus doux
> Qu'une nuit près de vous,
> Venez, venez jusqu'au bout de l'ombre;
> Là je vous tiens
> Si fragile en mes mains …
>
> Nothing is sweeter
> Than a night near you,
> Come, come to the edge of the dark.
> There I'll hold you
> So fragile in my hands...

As we reached the door I looked back to see the fragile hands of one of the ladies swing gaily along the stairway leading up to "heaven," as it was called, one of the customers, a plump little man, his bald head bouncing behind her like a tufted bowling ball.

I came back from the Sphinx, its sweet music still in my ears and still half-blinded by the entire dazzling city of light of which it seemed now to be the center, to the somber rue du Sommerard. There in the dark hallway I was greeted by the narrow orange glowworm band night switch that I knew, when pressed, would give me just light enough to get me to the top of the stairs and back to my room. I had managed previously to reach the light switch in my room before the light in the hallway went off. But this last night I was too tired and too distracted to move quickly, so when the light went out I found myself having to make my way down the hallway in pitch dark. I was terrified as I inched along the wall, finding nothing familiar to hold on to, moving forward at a snail's pace until my damp hand found the doorknob and below it the keyhole. The next problem was finding the light switch in the room. I moved forward now with some confidence, thinking that I was home safe and that my bed just a few feet away was awaiting me. My confidence was soon shaken when I felt what seemed to be a knife-blade cutting into my forehead just above my right eye. I had walked smack into the open door of the closet and the door's sharp edge had broken through my flesh. I reached up to feel the blood oozing out. I quickly staunched the bleeding but my head continued to throb: I had the sensation that it had been split open and that I was trying desperately to hold the two pieces together.

I fell into bed, my head pounding, and completely exhausted sank immediately into deep sleep making my way in a dream at the end of a long journey through a strange moonlit landscape down avenues of bearded oaks, the Spanish moss brushing my cheeks as I ambled along. At the end of the avenue under the tall white classical columns of a southern mansion stood my eighty-three-year-old grandmother.

"Come," she said, "I know that you have traveled a long way and you must be very tired." She led me to a great four-poster bed and left me on white pillows under a mosquito net.

No sooner had she departed than I found myself elegantly dressed in the middle of a great ballroom where any number of young women, one more beautiful than the next, clad in low-necked dazzling gowns waltzed past me. I was just about to take one of them in my arms to lead her across the floor when I heard my grandmother summon me again.

"Come to the window," she said, as she drew the curtains. "I never thought that I would live to see them grow so tall."

And there before us banks of immense house-high orange-gold nasturtiums rose inexplicably from the black bayou, and suddenly from their great tiger-red flowering trumpets came a steady shrill penetrating sound. It was my alarm clock. My head still throbbing I pulled on my clothes, threw everything in my suitcase, and stumbled down the stairs to stand for a few quiet minutes in the corner café with a cup of black coffee and a croissant, the crisp flavor of which gave me the courage to hail a cab and make my way to the station. The flesh above my eye was barely broken and the cut looked as if it had been drawn by a red pencil. Paris had left its mark on me and everyone in the Gare d'Orléans was staring at me, I thought, wondering what kind of brawl I had been in. It was a relief to find a seat on the train and to press my face to the glass and gaze out again on the pretty houses, the flowered balconies, and the green fields as we left Paris behind us.

III

The Garden

I don't think that I saw much as the train descended into the Loire Valley. I dozed off more than once but when I looked out at the river with its light green willows, clumps of shimmering poplars, and blond sand-bars I knew that I had reached my destination. The station at Tours was quiet and accommodating after Paris, and I was able to find my way without difficulty across town to the Institut de Touraine. The Institut looked like anything but a school: at the corner of the rue de Clocheville and the rue de la Grandière, it was a great town house, what the French call an *hôtel* of what seemed to me great elegance. Its main entrance was through grilled gates into a walled garden with gravel paths and benches and there opposite stood the façade of the Institut with circular steps leading up to a balcony with a stone balustrade. Through the windows I gazed in at a room with pale blue walls and a gilt mirror on one side above a marble fireplace. From the center of a gold-trimmed medallion hung a crystal chandelier. The ceiling itself was a pale blue sky with clouds and swallows sweeping across it. There were painted medallions above the doors. Across the parquet floor there were several rows of long desks reaching across the room with chairs behind them. On the opposite wall facing the mirror was the desk of the professor, and in one corner, the only mundane piece of equipment, a blackboard. In the hall near the office, I found a huge poster that read: ETUDIANTS, *venez à l'Institut de Touraine*, and there below pictures of some châteaux, *"au plus pur de la civilisation, de la langue, de la lumière, and des paysages, de France."* And that was where I was sure that I had come: to the purest civilization, the purest language, the purest light and the purest landscape of France.

I could see that Stuart was right that nothing very much was going to happen here but enough *had* happened over the centuries to keep me occupied and happy for the next several months.

Along the rue Sébastopol that I followed to the pension to which I had been assigned I passed gray and white stucco houses and white walls through the grilled gates of which I could see patches of courtyards paved with white stones. Here and there wisteria climbed a wall or an iron grill, its mauve blossoms tumbling into the street. Everything looked as if it had been prepared for a presentation, a stage set waiting for some great pageant: the stones in the courtyards, the brass knobs of the heavy doors, the brass nameplates, all were gleaming and bright, as if dusted for my inspection. The rue Sébastopol ended at the rue Roger Salengro, and there to the left at 45 bis, facing the Jardin des Prébendes, stood the house that was to be my home for the next two and a half months. Madame Biéron, who ran the pension, was a dark-skinned widow with dark, dancing eyes, a deep throaty voice and a ready laugh. She gave one the sense right off that she was in charge, firmly in charge, and that everything was to be done the way she wanted it done, but within the bounds that she set she wanted those who had come to enjoy themselves just as she did. Despite whatever difficulties had brought her to her present reduced circumstances (her husband, a civil servant, had died years before), she clearly felt that life was to be lived and enjoyed. Here she was at the center of France's purest civilization, and she spoke its purest language. The house was one that I had had described to me in any number of nineteenth-century novels: the high-ceilinged parlor, on which the shutters were closed during the day, was papered in a pattern of pink roses. There was an upright piano with music always on its music stand and bright brass candlesticks on either side of the music, chairs of brown and purple plush, their backs pinned with lace antimacassars, a hundred little square and oval frames scattered around on little tables, a thin dark marble fireplace blocked off with an iron medallion and surmounted by a huge white-framed mirror, which, in the evening when we gathered for coffee, reflected every vase, every flower, every tassel, every stitch but which somehow, even in the harsh ugly overhead light, gave off a sense of warmth despite the magnitude of the room's seemingly pointless clutter. Double doors opened into the dining room, just big enough for a long table with places for from six to eight people, which was just about what the house could hold. French windows opened out upon a small walled garden with trees at the back, flower beds along the sides, and a central section where a few old canvas lawn chairs were set out on the gravel.

The dining room was the gathering place, the focal point of the pension, and here Madame Biéron, in her flowery print dresses, presided with all the flourish of a *grande dame*. The food was not great but was ample and fresh, and was presented in several courses on pretty platters. An assortment of ordinary vegetables, sliced tomatoes, cucumbers, grated carrots, and lettuce was presented in such a way that made it look like food I had never tasted before. The colors, the flavors, the patterns, the courses blending one into the other all seemed fresh and new. But when the cuts of cold meat came on a platter with the center of each cut a dark blood-red, I was taken aback. I had never touched meat that looked so absolutely raw. I would take a piece on my plate and approach it from the less raw edges working in toward the center, which finally at the end I downed swiftly since I could see that that was the thing to do. With every course there were the two essentials, slices of crusty bread and carafes of red wine. Unaccustomed to wine with meals, I was hesitant also in approaching that, adding, as I saw the others do, a bit of water to each glass. The meals were in every way formal and in every way satisfying but they were only the means to an end, and that end was conversation. Madame Biéron opened as if with golden keys each new topic which like an unexplored room in a castle was revealing its treasures for the first time. Even the most banal topic seemed magical, especially when enunciated by Madame Biéron in her lucid sparkling French. It all seemed especially so to me because many of the words I was hearing used I was hearing for the first time: I had seen them often on the printed page but I had never heard them or had a chance to utter them myself. It was only once in a great while that a word came that I could not grasp at all and which would block the flow of the conversation until I could stop and ask what it was that was being discussed. I often had to laugh afterwards when I found out what I had failed to understand. More than once, these words were not French at all but English words or names pronounced in a French way that made them completely incomprehensible. I was baffled for quite a while by a conversation about a character whose name was *Per-shang*. When I discovered that it was General Pershing who had been mentioned, everything fell into place.

The mention of General Pershing prompted Madame Biéron, to my astonishment, to remark rather acidly that there were no longer any generals of the caliber of Pershing or Foch.

"Our generals these days," she said, "do nothing but sit around and boast about their magnificent creation, the Maginot Line, which, like the Great Wall of China, is supposed to keep invaders out forever."

Madame Biéron's French was perfection, but that of the others at the table left much to be desired, and the accents with which it was pronounced varied considerably. Everyone who appeared at the pension—and in the course of the summer there were representatives of several nations—had a good basic knowledge of the language and was able to carry on an ordinary conversation. Without some background and training and an interest in French language and culture, he or she would not have come so far and often at such expense. The faces at the table changed over the months but those that remained for the greater part of the time were those that greeted me on my arrival. The oldest and most prominent was that of Signorina Emilia Morandini, an old-maid school teacher from Milan. Signorina Emilia seemed never to leave the classroom: she took the greatest pleasure in correcting each of us. She spoke rapid-fire and she never stopped talking and made her corrections without pausing, simply giving quickly the proper idiom (she seemed a veritable idiomatic fountainhead) for the one that had been mangled and then went right ahead with her story or what appeared to be her lesson. Her French was, of course, impeccable, but with its *méridional* accent that seemed always to add a syllable to the nasal endings—as if the Italian *–mente* hovered behind every *–ment*—it had, beside the pure flow of Madame Biéron's, a somewhat tedious mechanical quality to it. And that quality was made even more evident by the shrill edge to her voice. Signorina Emilia was probably not more than fifty but the thin, frizzled, graying hair that she wore in narrow braids around her head made her appear at least ten years older. She usually wore black dresses or dark skirts and blouses that gave the impression of being black: they were always uniform without any variation of pattern or hint of color. She carried an old handbag of cracked, black leather, the size of a doctor's kit, in which she stuffed innumerable dog-eared notebooks containing, I suspected, thousands of idioms. Also from Italy but in sharp contrast to the Signorina was the young, round-faced Claudia Betocchi. Claudia almost never spoke, but when she did, it was in a soft musical voice. She had expressive green eyes and wore neatly ironed colorful cotton blouses. Claudia might have been one of Signorina Emilia's students but as such she was never corrected but constantly ignored: there were few exchanges between them at the table and even fewer when they left it. Beside the dark-skinned Italians were two very blond Swedes, Bo and Elvira, whose family names I never mastered. Bo was a short, stocky, very blond, very athletic young man who had a penchant for double-breasted suits and bright neckties. He looked always as if he had just walked off a tennis court and with his good humor and pleasant disposition and well-turned speech, he seemed destined for the diplomatic corps. It may well have been with that destination in mind that he had come to Tours. If Bo looked as if he had just come off the tennis court, Elvira looked as if she had been watching him, not from the grandstand but from the royal box. Tall and elegantly dressed, she had a regal air about her when she removed her dark glasses and her broad-brimmed straw hat and spoke in a soft but commanding voice as if she expected the gentlemen around her to serve her, as indeed in the future many were destined to do and as at the moment I would have willingly done. The one representative at our table from central Europe was Karl, a Czech from Prague. Of a good Roman Catholic, middle-class family, with his cool good looks and his ramrod stance, Karl looked like a soldier out of uniform, or, a civilian waiting and ready to become a soldier.

It did not seem possible that all the food that appeared at the table had been produced by little Marguerite, who not only prepared the food but served at the table and brought our breakfasts, big cups of *café au lait* and *petits pains*, up to our rooms. She had a broad freckled face, short light brown hair, and in her simple gingham dresses, clearly had come from somewhere deep in the country. She appeared to enjoy life just as much as Madame Biéron although it was hard to see how all the chores—cleaning, cooking, serving—left her time to enjoy anything.

My room in the front of the house on the second floor looked out on a little park that was the focal point of the neighborhood. The entrance consisted of two tall iron gates in a fence with lace-like grillwork set back in a semicircle from the street. (The entire park was enclosed in a grilled fence about half as high.) At the center of the lacy grillwork of each gate was an iron escutcheon with rolled edges holding a central plaque that, even though it bore no royal coat of arms, made the park seem positively regal. There may be little parks in this world more beautiful than the Jardin des Prébendes, as it was called, but I have yet to see them. If Touraine was the garden of France, then this was the garden within the garden, the many-faceted green center of a great emerald. With carefully planted beds of begonias, snapdragons, and petunias laid out in ornate patterns, and ivy-encircled huge cedars of Lebanon, it had several lily-scattered ponds edged by clumps of bamboo, through the dark waters of which swans sailed from ivy-clad islands like legendary vessels. The only sounds in the park, which I visited regularly, were the crunch of a few slow feet on the gravel paths, the slapping of the water as ducks slipped into it, the cooing of doves in the branches overhead, and the cries of little children along with the soothing voices of the mothers and grandmothers attending them: *"Viens avec moi . . . Ça va te faire mal."* Come, come with me, all the paths seemed to say, and the little wooden bridges arching over the water echoed them: come. The magic quality of the Jardin was enhanced by my discovery that the greater part of the statuary it contained honored poets and artists. To the left of the main entrance opposite my window was a white-marble bust of Pierre de Ronsard. The likeness of the poet, with his fine features, long thin nose, and delicate trimmed beard, under a moss-capped laurel wreath, was for me especially welcoming. Below the base on which it rested with its high collar and buttoned tunic, in cascading vine leaves, grapes at their edge, cupids played and tumbled against a magnolia tree in full bloom and over them I could hear the voice of the poet as he said to his young love, come,

> Mignonne, allons voir si la rose
> Que ce matin avait déclose
> Sa robe de pourpre au soleil . . .

And right there in the bright sunlight the rose had indeed opened its purple gown. As to the children, the voice said, Come, come and see. And with my head propped up on the bolster against my white linen pillow, I could hear the voice at night below my window. Come, it said: "Ceuillez dès aujourd'hui les roses de la vie." And that is exactly what I planned to do—seize the day and gather the roses of this life. I was young, active, open and ready, and I had come, as in a dream, to the garden of France, the garden of the world.

IV

The Universe

I started day by day to explore the streets of Tours and everything that I saw seemed to emanate harmony. My feet would follow along the white curbstone and my eye would catch all the pits and crevices, all the spider-web patterns in the cobble stones and then I would lift my eyes to the plane trees along the walk and find on their trunks spotted like the hides of giraffes the same patterns and then my eyes would rise still higher and discover in the clouds sailing along in a clear sky the identical patterns. I would watch the leaves of the poplars turning in the light and dancing, shimmering in the wind on the blond sands of the Loire. Victor Hugo called the poplar the silliest of trees, one that had, he said, "the dullness of the alexandrine." But to me the alexandrine had all the charm of Mozart's formal music and the leaves of the poplar were the quicksilver of a human heartbeat. To my eye the iron grillwork of a balcony against the white front of a house was a scroll of exquisite script or the score of a majestic symphony. A woman with a baguette under her arm on the rue Nationale was a princess whose wand pointed to the treasures in all the shops, the *pruneaux fourrés*, the *sucre d'orge*, the buckets of fresh fruit, the *reine-claudes*, the cascading flowers.

For centuries others before me had responded to the power of this place. Something almost miraculous had drawn people here since Roman times and even before. Saint Martin of Tours, who became the greatest bishop of the Gauls, began as a soldier in the Roman legion. One day at the gate of Amiens he came upon a beggar shivering in the cold and promptly with his sword cut his cloak in two and gave half of it to protect the poor man. In a dream the following night he had a vision of Christ wearing half his cloak. He was baptized and soon afterward at Ligugé in Poitou founded the first monastery in Gaul. In 372 he became the bishop of Tours and continued his fight against paganism. He built chapels and churches throughout Touraine, including the monastery of Marmoutier on the outskirts of Tours. He died in 397, and the basilica built a century later over his tomb in Tours attracted ordinary pilgrims drawn by the report of the miracles that had occurred there, as well as powerful princes seeking absolution from their crimes.

The metaphor of the cloak, suggesting comfort and protection, was more than once associated with the region. The historian Michelet called Touraine "a homespun cloak with golden fringes," the golden fringes being the wonderful fertile valley, but the cloak itself the harsh plateaux with their limestone deposits. I had grown up in the limestone country of Missouri, where water had worked its way through the stone with spectacular results. Here along the roadside throughout the valley in the white chalky deposits of *tufa* people had built their houses right into the hillside caverns. The resulting troglodyte residences with their elaborately embellished exteriors, with green lawns and trellised flower beds, appeared to have sprung fully finished from the earth itself.

At the heart of the city, the Cathedral of St-Gatien, with its towering Gothic presence, constructed of the white limestone that was present everywhere, its dark interior with stained glass windows, seemed also a monumental cavern, carved naturally from the porous landscape.

Modern Tours was an important commercial center and during the day its streets, especially the rue Nationale that divided the city down the middle, were busy with every sort of activity. We students soon got to know the shops with their rich variety. But as in many other provincial capitals everything shut down in the evening—the shops pulled down their shutters, the restaurants closed early, the people withdrew behind their walled gardens. There were not many cafés. And perhaps because of its location in the Jean Jaurès Square at the center of town opposite the Hôtel de Ville and the Palais de Justice, the terrace of the Hôtel de l'Univers, with its little round tables and its cane-backed chairs comfortably situated under the trees across from the fountain at the center of the square, was a delightful spot that very soon became the favorite gathering place for the foreign students of the Institut.

The Swedish contingent was always the first to arrive and the last to leave. It was headed by Bo from our pension with a commanding presence and great panache. He was usually joined by two or three of his handsome blond compatriots, all elegantly done up in jackets and ties, looking for all the world like young diplomats. They were joined by the English group, male and female, the young men in blazers and the young women in pretty summer dresses. There were fewer Americans, one or two, and then a sprinkling of other nationalities. There was no dress code but we were all eager to show that we knew our way around in the big world, which the Univers, as the most elegant hotel in Tours, represented. There was also a certain eagerness to display the best of the clothes we had brought with us since there were few other places where we could.

In the course of the evening people came and went, but a core of eight or ten of us settled in around three or four of the small tables. The conversation, which became more and more animated as the evening progressed, was anything but serious. We left behind the seriousness of the classroom and the lecture hall, determined to enjoy ourselves totally. We made fun of everything and took special pleasure in playing with the language that we had come there to master. We would bring forth in triumph the most outrageous examples of the slang we had just picked up:

"*Vous yoyotez de la touffe!*" (You have yoyos playing under your hairpiece: you are nuts.)

"*Vous charriez dans les bégonias.*" (You are piling it on—there in the begonia bed: you are exaggerating.)

And there always seemed to be an occasion to declare:

"*C'est la fin des haricots!*" (That's the last of the string beans: that's all we needed.)

We discussed what went on in our pensions and what had happened on our excursions to each château. Political subjects were in general avoided. And when this rule was broken once by someone introducing the subject of the abdication of Edward VIII, the English responded by attacking Mrs. Simpson, the woman for whom he had chosen to give up his throne. In the heated discussion that followed and cast a pall on the evening, I felt, as an American, called upon to defend my compatriot Wallis Simpson, about whom I really knew very little. People had told me that my mother looked like her or at least that my mother wore her hair in the same way that she did. But I thought that my mother was infinitely better looking and my heart was not in the defense. The more usual reference to nobility came in the song "*Tout va très bien, Madame la Marquise,*" which was popular then throughout France and which many of us knew by heart. The song seemed to characterize the carefree spirit of our gathering. It begins with Madame la Marquise on the telephone to the majordomo of her estate, asking how everything had been during the fortnight of her absence. James answers that except for the death of her gray mare, everything is just fine:

> Mais à part ça,
> Madame la Marquise
> Tout va très bien, Tout va très bien.

The Marquise gradually learns that everything was fine except that the gray mare had perished when the stables burned down, and everything was still fine except that the fire had started in the château, when her husband, who had been ruined financially, had committed suicide, and, in doing so, had accidentally set fire to the château, which burned to the ground. The song was one of those skillfully executed vaudeville turns, a house of cards elaborately built up so that it could come delightfully tumbling down. The conclusion which describes the husband falling finally and overturning the candles that started the disastrous fire is summed up very quickly. We all prided ourselves on knowing every word of it and being able to deliver it with the speed it required:

> Et c'est en ramassant la pell'
> Qu'il renversa tout's les chandell's,
> Mettant le feu à tout l'château
> Qui s'consuma de bas en haut;
> Le vent soufflant sur l'incendie
> Se propagea sur l'écurie
> Et c'est ainsi qu'en un moment
> On vit périr votre jument!
> Mais à part ça, Madame la Marquise,
> Tout va très bien, tout va très bien.

The *soucoupes* that had piled up on our tables clattered, the tables shook, we had brought down the house, and we beamed with delight: everything was just fine.

Joy was sweeping all of France that summer in the songs of Charles Trenet, the title of one of which was simply "There is joy (*Y'a d'la joie*)." It was a joy that only his French words could convey and that were lost in translation. "*Je chante*" was the title of another, and sing he did for all of us. Like the gray mare of Madame La Marquise, a horse was the ridiculous focus of one of his most popular pieces, "*Vous oubliez votre cheval.*" This creature had been left by mistake with the hatcheck girl in a restaurant, who complains to the customer from Toulouse in words that we all knew:

> Monsieur, monsieur
> Vous oubliez votre cheval
> Ne laissez pas cet animal
> Il y serait vraiment trop mal…

The texture of nonsense at the Univers became each evening more and more all enveloping the more we drank as the evening wore on. We really drank very little—nobody seemed to have much money—but we drank very slowly. It was the company more than the beer or the wine that intoxicated us. But the Swedes wanted us all the same to believe that it was the drink. They introduced us to a Swedish drinking song that appeared to be the culmination of nonsense. They sang it so often that I asked them to write the words down for me. As I copy them out now from the little notebook that I have kept, the quick merry notes that accompanied them seem to fly from the page:

> Helan går,
> Sjung, hopp fadderallan lej!
> Och den som inte helan tar,
> Han heller inte halvan får.
> Helan går!
> Sjung, hop fadderallan lej!

The song apparently advises the drinker to empty his glass in one gulp, for if he doesn't take the whole glass, he won't get the half either—and so he had better drink it down. And drink it down we did.

When we finished at the Univers, we set off still singing through the dark quiet streets around the corner to the train station and the Buffet de la Gare, which was always open. Here in the dark-walled interior whose brass fixtures caught the reflection of our laughing faces, we had a feast of Renaissance proportions. The menu never varied: Steak (if there had been a printed menu, it would have been spelled in the French way, *steack*), *pommes frites*, and *haricots verts*. Over the crowded tables the waiters deftly maneuvered their copious trays and the delicious aromas drifted, colored festive streamers, around the room. I have yet to encounter anywhere French-fried potatoes to equal those of the Buffet de la Gare. While their delicate salt smell rose to the nostrils, the thin crisp brown edges melted in the mouth. One did not consume those *frites*; they just melted away, a crisp-coated liquid gold, highlighting the dark-edged steak and its bloody-red interior. The accompanying wine and beer like the crimson and gold in the tapestries of the châteaux held together all the flavors of our feast.

As we made our way back to the center of town, where we parted company to go off to our various pensions, the English took the lead in showing us how to do the Lambeth Walk, the dance step that had become the craze on both sides of the Channel. We sang:

> Any time you're Lambeth way,
> Any evening any day,
> You'll find us all doin' the LAMBETH WALK
>
> Ev'ry little Lambeth gal
> With her little Lambeth pal
> You'll find us all doin' the LAMBETH WALK

As we sang, we would link our arms, step to the side and back, then separate and slap our knees in time to the music, ending by pointing our thumbs in hitch-hike fashion over our shoulders and yelling, "Hey!" That exclamation seemed the fitting conclusion to a truly memorable evening.

While the participants in these evenings were, for the most part, foreigners who were all students at the Institut, there were also a few students from our host country taking summer courses at the branch of the University of Poitiers in Tours who joined us. One of them, accompanied by a younger friend, soon became a regular member of the group. She had at first seemed so modest and retiring, seated always on the side and rarely joining in the main conversation, more often turning to whisper to her companion, that I had scarcely noticed her. With her light golden brown hair and her dark gray sweater crisscrossed with gold thread, she was lovely, but the last thing she wanted to do was to assert herself unduly. As time went by and she became more and more a part of the inner circle, it happened that one night she was seated right next to me. I began to examine her more closely and saw for the first time how really beautiful she was. She had the kind of beauty that Renoir had captured in his paintings—skin that was so like porcelain that it gave her full face, and fully rounded body a fragility so great that it seemed ready to break with any sudden gesture or abrupt movement. Her rich contralto voice gave one the immediate sense that her fragile exterior was shored up by a strong, dark, and mysterious inner force. Her name was Diane Davril. As the evening progressed and we made our way with the group to the Buffet de la Gare, in between the choruses of the songs, I learned more and more about her. A native of Bourges, she was enrolled in the medical school of the University of Poitiers. Her father was a dentist, and she herself was studying to follow in his footsteps. She had spent the previous summer studying in London and was fluent in English. On the way back to the main square, she was my partner doing the Lambeth Walk, the steps of which she executed with great verve. When we parted from the others at the place Jean Jaurès, we turned together down the dark tree-lined and deserted boulevard Béranger and stopped to sit on one of the benches in almost total darkness. No sooner were we seated than we fell into each other's arms and after several lengthy passionate embraces, began at once to tell each other the stories of our lives. A plethora of relevant and irrelevant facts came pouring forth. Much of what we said was deeply felt and well stated; much of it was awkward and silly. But we each seemed to want to get it all out as if, although this was our first time together, it might well be our last, as if there would be no tomorrow. This exchange became so rapid and heated that I gave up trying to express myself in French and turned to English, which Diane understood perfectly and answered me with a steady flow of French, which I also understood. This bilingual back-and-forth became the usual pattern for our most intense moments. For the more relaxed and ordinary conversation, we both went on in French. We soon found many things in common: she had a sister a year and half younger; they were totally different and did not get along. Like her sister my brother was a year and half younger and might well have been from another planet we were so unalike. She and I both liked learning a language other than our own—we wanted to know all that we could about our own countries but we also wanted to see and know something of the rest of the world. We covered a great deal of territory in this initial conversation but it was really quite brief. In a few minutes we were convinced that we were made for each other. Because Diane had to be up early the next morning I saw her back to her pension on the rue Victor Hugo, kissed her good night, and turned down the rue Sébastopol to find my own bed. I stumbled along in a total daze and climbed the stairs to my room as if I were walking in my sleep and about to tumble over a precipice. I gazed down at the grilled gate of the Jardin des Prébendes and at the bust of Ronsard just beyond it, clearly outlined in the moonlight. I had like the poet now found my *mignonne*. But was she really my darling? Or was it all a dream and would her pink porcelain vision shatter in the cold light of dawn? I drifted off to sleep, as if drugged by the memory of the scent of roses and the memory of her perfume.

Her carefully timed appearance the following evening at the Univers, a slight, knowing nod and a flash of her china-blue eyes, gave me absolute assurance that she was indeed real, however fragile she seemed. At the end of the evening we made our way to our dark bench on the boulevard Béranger, to an even more passionate embrace and to a long dialogue that continued until the early hours of the morning. Our evenings continued like this on through the month of June and into July. We were, of course, merely "necking," as such kissing and caressing was called at the time when amorous play, no matter how intense, did not, for young women of good standing necessarily lead immediately to bed. But our encounters all the same represented for us a powerful passionate and enduring commitment. I came to know what Emily Dickinson meant when she wrote, *Wild nights! Wild nights!* about the encounters with her beloved Judge Lord in her dark front parlor. I was so in love that I was in a state of constant ecstasy and torment. I couldn't wait to see her and when I saw her I wanted our meeting never to end and yet at the same time I couldn't wait for it to end so that I might have her wholly in my memory. And the thought of her colored every moment of my school day. I particularly enjoyed the sessions of phonetics because the phonetic symbols became for me a kind of secret code by which to transmit my love. I wrote her long imaginary letters in this code, and then I wrote real letters to her in answer to those that she wrote to me. Often when I came back in the late afternoon, one of her letters would be awaiting me—letters that she herself had delivered written on beautiful blue notepaper in her exquisite hand. Each one bore beneath the address on the envelope the capital letters E.V., meaning "En Ville." When I discovered what E.V. stood for, I was puzzled: where indeed could I be, if not in the city? We met with the others at the Univers, but on our own sometimes in the late afternoon for tea in a delicious pastry shop on the rue Nationale, that had every color and shape of delicious pastry, cakes of every description, and myriads of jeweled petits-fours. We also went out of Tours on more than one occasion, once to the nearby village of Vouvray at the heart of the famous vineyard on the north bank of the Loire where near some delightful troglodyte houses, we visited the cave hollowed deep into the limestone cliff and we sampled the dry mellow white wine made from the Chenin blanc grape, called locally the *Pineau de la Loire*. The large group of students made this a joyous occasion with toasts and laughter and gave us the feeling that we were part of the *confréries vineuses*, the wine producer's brotherhoods, which over the centuries had introduced new chevaliers to their ranks. Lifting the *vouvray pétillant*, as clear and sparkling as the sun on the sandbanks of the Loire, we allowed ourselves to say, as the French do, *"Cela se laisse boire,"*—"That is drinkable." And drinkable indeed it was.

The Loire valley is watered by innumerable rivers, rivulets, and streams. One of the most delightful of these that winds through the valley is the river Cher, on which the château of Chenonceaux rests.

On a gorgeous sunny day we left the town behind us and

started off through the fields that Diane knew so well. We were soon in the midst of a world of gold and green where we passed peach orchards and wheat fields edged with Queen Anne's lace and white butterflies circling the tall grass. And we soon found ourselves at a secluded spot where the river Cher was narrow and calm and as clear and bubbly as the Vouvray we had drunk some days before.

On one bank a row of poplars stood reflected in the green water, their trunks outlined against a golden field on which the light played in the distance; on the other a willow trailed its branches down to the water's edge. Beyond them clumps of moss and cress swept out to form a kind of pale green water meadow that parted like the strands of a delicate curtain as we swam. We were not naked, but I felt as if we were. The cool water rippling over Diane's white skin in the dappled shade as she floated along on this water-meadow made her a veritable emanation of the stream, a spirit that came alive in this water world. When I touched her body in the water it was as if I had grasped the transparent light itself, rippling through my fingers and flowing with an equal transparency through my whole body. The hours that we spent wheeling, cavorting, laughing went quickly by and the sun was beginning to set when we started back to town. Along the darkening path we seemed to be still dividing the water meadow. When we met again that night with the other students at the Univers her crystalline laughter brought back the enchantment of the afternoon, and when I kissed her goodnight at her pension, and got back to my room, it was still with me. As I dozed off I started a poem:

> Oh, I remember swimming in the Cher,
> Light filtering down through the trees…

That is as far as I got that night, but those lines would return to me on more than one occasion.

V

La Touraine: Cloud Castles

In a soft blue sky white clouds appear:
The days grow longer, summer's here;
We lie in the shade by bubbling streams
And build cloud castles in our dreams.

Since Diane was often occupied with classes in the afternoon, I began on my own to explore the riches of the countryside. Or rather, not on my own but in the company of one of my classmates, Chester Matthews from Philadelphia. Chester was an awkward affable young fellow with a sandy bristling crew cut that accentuated his square face. He was a junior, majoring in French at Haverford, and it was clear that he came from a family of some means. He had excellent manners but execrable French, which he insisted on speaking most of the time. His written French was tolerable but when he spoke it was as if his tongue were making its way around the cobblestones of his native city. We had met early on at the Institut and wherever I turned during the day, he was there beside me, ready with the latest bit of practical information: he knew where to find everything that any student could possibly need; he knew how much it cost and whatever discount we as students could claim. He seemed to be good at everything I was bad at and so we complemented each other. When he proposed that we go cycling together to visit the châteaux, I agreed at once. He found us the best bicycles to rent at the best price and he always knew the best and shortest way to any château we chose to visit: he was acute and accurate at reading road maps and road signs. He was really a great help, and since he was so adept at getting us where we wanted to go, I decided to grind my teeth and endure the French that he fractured so thoroughly.

I knew that the châteaux of the Loire that we set out to visit were not technically "castles." The word "castle" should be translated by *"château-fort,"* that fortified feudal dwelling surrounded by moats, walls and towers enclosing a dungeon or keep and usually situated, like an eagle's aerie, atop almost inaccessible rocks. The *château-fort* derived from the Carolingian château, which in turn was the transformation of a Roman villa. The Valois tried, often with considerable success, to unite the fortified Medieval château with the Renaissance palace. The word *château* had come by extension to mean a lordly dwelling, of which in Touraine there were all shapes and sizes. I knew this very well, but all the same I was so much in love that every château, whether rising however modestly beside the water or enveloped in the haze of a far-off hillside, became at once a castle of a sort that evoked the tales of Perrault or Madame d'Aulnoy. And as we cycled over fields and streams, I began, like Quixote, to imagine cloud castles even more fabulous than those that awaited us. But Chester Matthews, my Sancho Panza, was always there to bring me back, in his flat-footed way, to base reality.

"C'est magni - fi - que!" he exclaimed, drawing out the *fi* into an elongated diphthong *ee - ee*, making his statement far more of a shriek than an exclamation.

We were approaching the château of Chenonceaux down the long allée of plane trees bordered by moats on either side. It was here, our guidebook told us, that Catherine de Médicis had celebrated the arrival of François II and Mary Stuart on 3 March 1560 and for the first two weeks of April 1563, that of Charles IX, in a most elaborate fashion. On the latter occasion young women disguised as mermaids emerged singing from the moats to greet the guests; their song was echoed by nymphs coming from the neighboring wood, with satyrs in hot pursuit. For four days delight followed delight; there were dances, masquerades, excursions on the water, naval combats, and visits to an aviary, where Catherine had gathered flocks of rare birds.

At the end of the green allée, as it had for those guests centuries before, Chenonceaux rose for us in all its white splendor. A rare bird itself, it perched on the edge of the Cher, its body and its tail resting on the water and stretching out to the other side of the river.

When Henri II came to the throne in 1547, he gave Chenonceaux, which François I had used as a hunting lodge, to his mistress Diane de Poitiers. She began immediately, with the help of Philibert de l'Orme, who had distinguished himself at Fontainebleau and at her other château d'Anet, to design the garden. Set out Italian style, protected by an embankment to prevent it from flooding, and connected to the château by a wooden bridge over the moat, it was laid out in compartments converging at the center on a fountain with a jet of water eighteen feet high. Philibert de l'Orme also designed for her the stone bridge with a gallery on top connecting the château to the south bank of the Cher. Only the pillars of the bridge had been completed when Henri II was killed in a tournament, speared by Montgomery of his Scotguard. The wife of Henri II, Catherine de Médicis, completed the gallery we saw that day and she also took her revenge on her rival Diane by ordering her to give up Chenonceaux in exchange for the more ordinary and forbidding château of Chaumont.

Of all the women who exercised power over the Valois monarchs, Diane de Poitiers was the most extraordinary. She was twenty years older than Henri II, but her beauty was such in the words of Brantôme, that "her winter was more glorious than the spring and summer of any other." She had preserved her beauty with great care: on a pure white skin of delicate transparency, she never wore make-up of any sort. It was the cold clear water of the Cher that kept her young and supple: she followed her early rides through the park with cold baths. She was the widow of Louis de Brèze, the grandson of Charles VII. On his death in 1531 she went into mourning, wearing only black and white, and when she became Henri's mistress, those became the court's colors and hence also the colors of the tiles she chose for the floor of the gallery spanning the river. As we made our way through the vaulted and groined entrance hall of Chenonceaux and through the high ceilinged rooms with their elegant fireplaces, I had the impression that we were being led by Diane de Poitiers herself. She wore a black velvet gown trimmed in ermine, and her hair with its glint of gold was decked out with jewels in the elaborate coiffure of the period. At her side was Henri II in pourpoint of black velvet slashed with white satin and followed by the royal pages in their costumes of black satin and white leather, with Diane's symbol of interlacing crescents stitched in silver on their sleeves. Diana the huntress with her bow and arrow, her stag and her dogs, was also Diana-Artemis, the moon-goddess whose crescent identified her with the moon. Ronsard vowed to call attention to the crescent when one day he honored her all-powerful name in an immortal poem. Diane resolved "to clothe her thoughts as carefully as her body," and by awakening in Henri II and his court an interest in the arts, she became the very symbol of the Renaissance that had begun to touch every aspect of life in Touraine.

So honored and powerful did Diane become and so influential in every decision of Henri II that she created a device linking her initials with his in what became the royal cipher that was widely displayed:

As we left Chenonceaux behind us and cycled back along the Cher, I carried in my mind the imprint of that cipher, and I found that my bicycle tires began to trace it in the dust of the roads we followed. If Henri had his Diane, I had mine and she had the same initials, and what would be simpler, I thought, preparing a device for our lasting love, than to move the D's a bit farther apart, thus forming a W (for my William):

I thought of Diane de Poitiers reclining on the bed in what was supposedly her bedchamber, the rear room to the left overlooking the river, opposite the fireplace designed by Jean Goujon, who had also immortalized her in sculpture. I pictured her there as the painter Francesco Primaticcio had. For him she was Diane, the Huntress, lying languorously nude on a hillside under a tree, her arms resting affectionately on the stag kneeling beside her. The nipples of her breast stood out as firm as if she had just emerged from one of her cold baths and as firm as those of Diane Davril when I touched them the night before and as they had stood out the afternoon we bathed in the clear water of the Cher. I went to bed that night with a vision of the Huntress Diane just back from a ride through the forest, her white palfrey brushing through fields of yellow broom (the plantagenet that had given its name to the line of English monarchs) while the crescent moon hung caught in the tall poplars by the river as she galloped along. And I thought, as Rabelais had, that God must be a Frenchman to have created a province as pleasant as Touraine.

Our next excursion was to Blois and it proved to be a somber contrast to the dazzling whiteness of Chenonceaux. Victor Hugo loved Blois and when he first visited it as a young man he described it to his friend Alfred de Vigny as a haphazard city displaying "a thousand wonders, all at once: a disorderly confused mass of houses, bell towers, a château and a hill crowded with shadows."

As we proceeded up through the shadows of that hill, and into the courtyard of the château, we felt that we were going right to the center of the flamboyant beauty of the Renaissance and all the drama that surrounded it. The immediate effect of the octagonal, spiral staircase, the jewel built by François I, was so intense that it left Chester, always ready with his wildly pronounced exclamation, this time speechless. But he soon recovered, to mutter: *"C'est extra - ordinaire!"* How extra-ordinary it was we were soon to discover. The staircase, which resembled an open accordion standing on end, seemed to cut through the shadows and take us immediately into a world of mystery and intrigue.

The staircase was apparently designed for great receptions: the wall, three faces of which are recessed into one building and open between the buttresses, forms a series of balconies from which the court could contemplate the arrival of important persons. The columns are richly decorated with typical Renaissance designs of shells, putti, satyrs and horns of plenty. Above the doors is the crest of François I, the salamander with its head turned back and flame pouring from its open mouth. It stands with its front paw extended under a crown decorated with fleurs-de-lys and inscribed with the motto: *"Nutrisco et extinguo"* (I nourish and I extinguish). That device took on a special meaning as we climbed the stairs and moved deeper into the shadows of this haunted building to the first-floor bedroom of Catherine de Médicis. The adjoining study is lined with 237 wood panels carved in the Italian style, many of them hiding secret cupboards, which can be opened by pressing pedals on the skirting board. But it was on the floor above in the king's apartments that the entire tragic history of the place was revealed. It was here on the morning of 23 December 1588 that Henri de Lorraine, the duc de Guise, cousin and rival of Henri III, was assassinated.

The duke, head of the Catholic League in the Wars of Religion that were then sweeping France, had gained tremendous power in the north while the Loire Valley remained a bastion of Protestantism. In 1588 when the duke had taken control of Paris, his triumph prompted Henri III to call a meeting of the Etats généraux at Blois in November. At this gathering he swore that he and Henri de Guise would settle their differences. He would no longer attempt a reconciliation with the Protestants and Roman Catholicism would be the only religion in France. But in no more than a month, Henri, noted for changing his mind more frequently than any woman ever did, decided to break his oath. On 22 December, our guide told us, when the duke, who was visiting Blois, sat down to dine, he was handed a napkin that contained a message. "Take care," it read, "someone is about to do you harm." The duke read the note, and remarking at once, "No one would dare," threw it under the table and went off to spend the night with one of the lovely ladies of Catherine de Médicis's entourage. He rose early and was told that the king wanted to see him. He went to the Council Room, where he warmed his hands in front of the fire and ate one of the prunes in the comfit box that he carried. The king's secretary came to tell him that the king wished to see him in his old cabinet. In order to reach it, he had to go through the king's chamber where he found the assassins awaiting him. To escape from them, he turned toward the corridor, opened the door, and in the narrow passageway found the king's other men. They fell on him, seizing his arms and legs and wrapping his sword in his cloak. The duke, a big man, over six feet in height, knocked down four of his assailants, and wounding a fifth with his comfit box, staggered into the king's chamber, where he collapsed by the king's bed. Henri III stepped out from behind the tapestry and walked over to his rival.

"What a big fellow!" the king exclaimed, adding, as an afterthought, "larger in death perhaps than in life."

"And what did the king do then?" our guide asked. "Why, he went right down the secret stairway to tell his mother. He was queer, you know, a mother's boy, and he adored his mother, Catherine de Médicis. And she was certainly a pretty tough customer who prided herself on controlling everything. She was the one who had ordered the infamous massacre of thousands of Protestants on St. Bartholomew's Eve."

"Now, I am truly king of France," he told her, "the king of Paris is dead."

"I hope to God," she replied, "that you will not become king of nothing at all."

The next day the brother of Henri de Guise, the Cardinal of Lorraine, was also assassinated. The two bodies were burned and their ashes thrown into the Loire.

Henri III did not live much longer himself. The following year, as he sat one day on his commode, he was stabbed by a fanatic Dominican monk, who had come to take his revenge for the king's murder of Henri de Guise.

"Henri III, the last of the Valois kings," in the words of Morris Bishop, "possessed the perverse charm which clings to last things, the bright flush which hides the secret decay. . . . He loved his clothes, his jewels: he wore coquettish ear-pendants as well as rings, and fixed pearls in his elaborate coiffure. He introduced neck-ruffs so wide that spoons had to be made with longer handles. He was richly perfumed: his hair was besprent

with a powder of violet musk. Such powder was then made with a base of fine starch: one may picture His Majesty crowned with an aureole of flies. He pomaded his face, rouged his cheeks, and dangled a fan. He carried a bilboquet, a cup-and-ball, to beguile the tedious hours of duty.... As he grew older the court resounded with the King's scandalous affection for his mignons, the young gentlemen who formed his bodyguard. The mignons, fearing nothing from public opinion, rivaled their master in effeminacy. They wore their hair long and elaborately curled, billowing above tiny feathered hats precariously perched. Their starched and fluted ruffs were a half-foot wide, so that people said their heads looked like that of Saint John the Baptist served up on its platter."

"*Mon dieu...Quelle histoire!*" Chester exclaimed as we descended the spiral staircase into the bright sunlight.

"*Henri Trois, c'était un sale pédé*, a dirty faggot, *un vrai salaud.*" Chester seemed so pleased to have found the right words in French that he turned them right back into English," "a nasty queer little bastard, a real son-of-a-bitch."

As we descended the hill and left the shadows of that courtyard behind us, I had the impression that we had witnessed the dramatic enactment of a single episode in one of the many wars that for centuries had bloodied the banks of the clear streams in this garden of France. Had we, I wondered, seen the end of those wars? I had a distinct premonition of the dark clouds of an even greater conflict that were gathering then on the edge of the horizon, clouds that would darken forever the sunny streets where that summer we danced and sang.

As we cycled back to Tours the verse that I had begun so jubilantly after the sun-drenched afternoon with Diane, and that had returned triumphantly on the river's edge at Chenonceaux, now found its conclusion in the shadows of Blois:

> Oh, I remember swimming in the Cher,
> Light filtering down through the trees...

to which I now added, as we moved along:

> The perilous passageway at Blois
> And the murder of Henri de Guise.

With the historic nightmare of Blois behind me, I looked forward eagerly to my next encounter the following evening with Diane, and to the ever-present continuing dream of our love for each other that it represented.

She arrived as beautiful as ever at the Univers, and after a brief visit with our friends there, we were once again on the dark bench that we knew so well a few blocks away. But after a very short while in each other's arms, she came out with a remark so bizarre and unexpected that it cut right through that dream and brought us back abruptly, like one of Chester's odd observations, to base reality.

She drew back and in an almost accusatory tone, said, *"Tu as la tête d'un phoque."* (You look like a seal.)

I couldn't, for the life of me, make out what she meant. In all my moments of self-contemplation, of which there had been many, I would never have chosen as my totem animal the seal.

"What do you mean?" I stammered.

Diane's answer was to run her fingers through my sleek black hair and then down around the smooth contours of my face:

"All that."

Then I realized that she had seen something that I had never touched on in our conversations. Not long before I had come to France I had discovered that I had Native American, Choctaw, blood in my veins, which came from my mother's side of the family. Her elder sister had withheld this information from everyone because she feared that people might take such a mixture to be not of Choctaw, but of Negro, blood. When my mother discovered this fact on her own, she was proud to find that she was profoundly American, and, so was I. This heritage explained not only my jet-black hair, and my slightly Oriental eyes with their black pupils, but also my light beard that then consisted of only the slightest fuzz above my lips and on my chin.

When I explained to Diane what it was that she may have been referring to, she seemed not only satisfied, but delighted. Still it made me uneasy to think that the great differences in our backgrounds might in any way keep us apart.

I cannot now recall in what order Chester and I visited the châteaux, but it is to Chinon that my memory most often returns. It may well be because most of Chinon is in ruins and one's imagination must fill in all that is missing. What is left of its great wall stretches along the river Vienne high above the Medieval town. This long wall is made up of three fortresses

separated by huge moats, St. George's Fort, of which only the crypt remains, the Middle Castle with the restored clock tower, and the royal lodging, and on the end of the rocky spur, Coudray Fort.

In the eleventh century this fortress belonging to the counts of Blois had been taken over by their enemies the counts of Anjou. One of them, Henry Plantagenet, who in 1154 became king of England, had built the major part of it. Chinon always remained one of his favorite residences.

It was John Lackland, who on the death of his elder brother Richard the Lionheart, lost the Plantagenet Empire in the early thirteenth century, but the Hundred Years War (1337–1453) brought the English back. They gained control of half the country, and if Orléans had surrendered, would probably have taken over the rest. To keep them from doing so, Joan of Arc then announced her intention of driving the English out. The little shepherdess from Domrémy persuaded Charles VII to give her command of a little army, and with it she freed the beleaguered city of Orléans and put the English to flight in June 1429. In March of that year she had arrived in Chinon and had spent the first two days at an inn below fasting and praying, waiting to see the king.

When the eighteen-year-old girl was admitted to the palace, the king's entourage, suspicious of her intent, attempted at first to deceive her. Today only the west wall, with its famous fireplace, remains of the great hall that she entered on 9 March 1429. It was then lit by fifty torches and around them some three hundred gentlemen of the court had gathered. The king stood among them, dressed like the others, while one of his courtiers, wearing his robes, assumed his place. As we stood next to the fireplace, the clouds massed behind the clock tower above us, I pictured the torch-lit faces that had once surrounded it. Joan was not deceived: she moved slowly through the crowd and, ignoring the courtier wearing the king's robes, picked out the real king and went straight to him.

"Gentle Dauphin," she said, for to her, not having yet been crowned, he was still the Dauphin, "the King of Heaven has sent me to tell you that you will be anointed and crowned in the city of Rheims."

Charles, who had doubts about his legitimacy, was pleased to hear that this heaven-sent maid had found him to be the true son of the king, and he was ready at once to believe in her mission. But the king's advisers were still doubtful and Joan was made to appear in Poitiers before a panel of learned doctors, who were to decide whether she was bewitched or truly heaven-

William Jay Smith
in 1938

Diane Davril
(Madeleine Dufay)

Farewell party on the *S.S. Champlain* on the eve of arrival in Le Havre. *To the right* in the rear is WJS in a white jacket with black bow-tie. Immediately below him *right to left* are his dinner partners, Jacqueline Dumont, Professor Alberto Trova, and Janet Cleveland.

The pension on rue Roger Salengro, Tours, where WTS stayed. His room was on the second floor *on the right*.

Bust of the poet Pierre de Ronsard, Place du Maréchal Bertholot, in front of the Collège de France, Paris.

The Institut de Touraine, Tours.

Students in the parlor of the pension. Clockwise *left to right*: Karl, WJS, Claudia Betocchi, Emilia Morandini, Madame Biéron, Bo.

The entrance to the Jardin des Prébendes, as seen from WJS's window.

A student group ready to celebrate after a visit to the Caves.

Students on a bridge in the Jardin des Prébendes with Madame Biéron in the middle and WJS behind.

Swedish students at a table on the terrace of the Hôtel de l'Univers.

Madame Biéron under her umbrella at the pension.

On the terrace at the Hôtel de l'Univers. *To the right*, WJS in profile, with Diane (Madeleine) *on his left*, facing the table.

Diane (Madeleine) standing in the Jardin de Prébendes, photograph sent to WJS.

Karl, Czech friend of WJS, on the rocks at Le Croisic, August 1938.

Postcard sent by Diane (Madeleine) urging WJS to join her in La Baule.

Photograph sent to WJS by Diane (Madeleine). Chunks of ice in the Loire, she said, looked like water lilies on a lake.

WJS with his father at Schofield Barracks, Oahu, early June 1942.

WJS at Waikiki, June 1942 with his roommate and his roommate's Hawaiian girlfriend.

 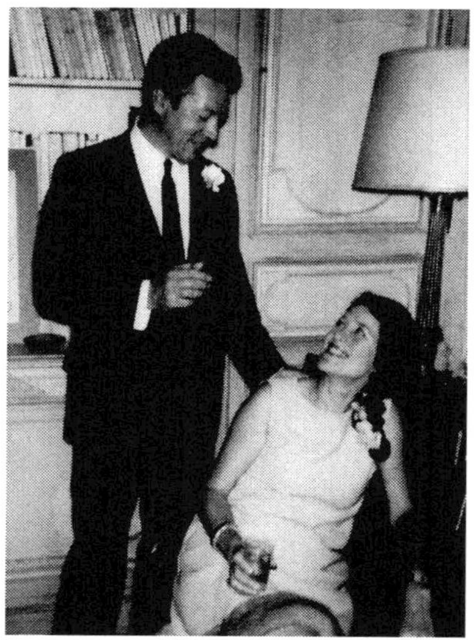

Sonja Haussmann Smith, in August 1995, seated before the Hôtel Royal, La Baule, where WJS and Diane (Madeleine) had sat in 1938.

WJS and his wife Sonja Haussmann after their marriage in Paris, 3 September 1966.

WJS, in August 1995, above the rocks of Le Croisic beside the hotel where he and Karl had stayed in 1938.

sent. With her naive but forceful replies to their demanding questions, she managed to convince them that she was indeed the "Messenger of God." She returned to Chinon, and left as the head of her little army on 20 April 1429.

As we cycled back through the forest of Chinon, the tall ferns reaching almost to our handlebars, I pictured the scene in that great hall, giant shadows cast on the walls, the glazed eyes of the courtiers, the simple pure face of the passionate maid and her tragic destiny, the flickering torches and wild flames that would ultimately consume the maid of Orléans when she burned at the stake.

"Have you ever thought," Chester asked when we pulled over at one point to rest, "how it would be now if Joan of Arc had stayed at home and looked after her sheep?"

And without waiting for my response, he answered his own question, this time so excited that he spoke breathlessly in English rather than in his fractured French.

"Why, the English would have taken Orléans and probably the rest of what is now France. The Plantagenets would have returned and the language on both sides of the Channel would have been French, and you know what . . . ?"

"What?"

"The Colonists who came to America would have spoken French and you and I wouldn't have had to learn that language, we'd have known it already."

He paused, adding with his deplorable accent, "*Ça, c'est vrai, n'est-ce pas, mon ami?*"

"*Certainement,*" I replied, dumfounded to think that Joan of Arc, if viewed in this way, might rightly be considered not as a saint but as a catastrophe.

Diane went home to Bourges to spend a few days with her parents, and I turned my attention to the Institut. But without her my mind wandered during the long sessions, the lectures, and the daily *dictées*. With one group we were translating Stevenson's *Dr. Jekyll and Mr. Hyde* into French, and fascinating though it was, the translation was tedious and slow. The phonetic sessions went very well: I enjoyed transcribing the French sounds into the phonetic symbols, which continued to be a kind of secret code that could cloak my innermost thoughts.

As we walked together to the Institut each morning, Signorina Emilia, quizzing me on a number of idioms, warned me that if I didn't spend more time studying each evening, I would not be prepared for the examinations. Was there a touch of jealousy in her admonition, I wondered, as I watched her heavy worn black bag swing along beside me.

When we left the dinner table and assembled in the parlor, I often sat down on the sofa beside Signorina Emilia while she sipped her coffee. And after a while, when I got up and excused myself, she seemed chagrined that I did not stay longer to discuss the beauties of Touraine and the complexities of the French language. She had appeared especially sad one evening when she had made a rare personal reference to her home life in Milan and to the little apartment that she shared with her aged mother, who would often in the evening spend hours combing her daughter's hair. She rummaged in her bag for a handkerchief, which she held up in a lonely gesture as if she were waving to someone from a great distance. I wanted to tell her how happy I was and to assure her that she could also be happy if she would not worry so much about every little thing, but I realized that the only way that I could make her happy was to show that I was slowly, but surely, mastering the French language that she loved so dearly and to sit with her for the rest of the evening, which I was not prepared to do.

When Diane returned, we resumed our passionate evenings together. I was so happy that I wanted somehow to celebrate, to give a big party and invite all my friends from the Institut and from the pension and from our gatherings at the Univers so that I might share my joy with them all. The city of Tours at just that moment came up with a celebration more splendid than any that I could have imagined and I felt that it had been planned just for me. For France's great holiday, the annual

Quatorze Juillet, celebrating the storming of the Bastille and the beginning of the French Revolution, a grandstand had been erected all along the Hôtel de Ville. I arrived early and found Diane with her English friend Joan, whom I had met in classes at the Institut, already there. Her gold-brown hair shining in the sun, Diane wore a simple white dress with a scarf imprinted with red and blue swirling patterns looped around her throat. Her friend Joan, tall and thin, looked like a belted white asparagus, topped with a floppy straw hat, and dark sunglasses set against her pale skin.

I hadn't seen any soldiers anywhere during our bicycle excursions, but they must have been hidden away in the landscape somewhere because on that day they all came marching out with great fanfare. There were military bands, drummers, buglers, and squads of quick-stepping soldiers, their uniforms immaculate, and officers, gold epaulettes on their shoulders and their gold-encircled *képis* straight on their heads.

There was a cavalry academy at Saumur, not far from Tours, that had been established in the eighteenth century by a crack regiment of the best horsemen in the Army, and a good many of the cadets from that academy must have been there, their horses richly caparisoned and their sabers flashing. There were squadrons of plumed hussars and tall black Senegalese. There were also the blue-uniformed gendarmes and a unit of the fire brigade of Touraine. There were standard-bearers proudly displaying their blue, white, and red tasseled standards. There were rows of bayonets, plumed helmets, white sashes, trucks and armored vehicles loaded with mysterious shining equipment, and lethal-looking dark green cannon rolling past, and everywhere proudly unfurled, the French tri-color, blue, white, red. It was a dazzling spectacle and the crowd time after time shouted its complete approval. There was such a fine festive spirit in the air that I felt like singing along with Charles Trenet, as we walked afterwards down the rue Nationale, in celebration of the joy of living. Why shouldn't there be pomp and ceremony, flags flying, bugles blaring? Joy indeed seemed to be everywhere that summer and we were, there in the garden of France, at the very heart of it.

We carried our mood of celebration, the four of us, Diane, Joan, her English companion Gregory, and I, into the tearoom on the rue Nationale that all the English-speaking students at the Institut referred to as "The Five O'clock," since it was the establishment that claimed to offer up *"le five o'clock à toute heure."*

The tea and cakes had no sooner arrived than Joan, who had never stopped talking all afternoon, even during the height of the parade, launched into a discussion of Lamartine's poem "Le Lac," about which she and Gregory and I had heard a lecture a few days before. Like so many of the English Joan was so fearful of a lull in the conversation, a vacuum that silence would rush in to fill, that she spoke as quickly as possible, introducing from time to time bits of utter nonsense rather than come to a complete halt. Listening to her made me dizzy, and I longed to be out on a lake somewhere in total silence.

She had removed her hat and dark glasses and spoke non-stop lickety-split in English with little bits of French sprinkled here and there like poppies in a wheat field:

"He's such a dear, isn't he, Professor Lancôme with his *pince-nez* and that *faux-col*, his striped trousers, and that great paunch jutting out over the edge of the lecture platform? I always feel that I'm dangling from that gold watch chain on his waistcoat as he takes us off on his literary journeys, don't you?"

She shot a glance at Gregory, who seemed himself to be dangling somewhere far off as she nervously rushed on: "He was just so wonderful when he quoted Lamartine:

> Ne pourrons-nous jamais sur l'océan des âges
> Jeter l'ancre un seul jour?

He had me there—I was in tears, honestly…

> O temps, suspends ton vol!

That really *stopped* me. *Comme poésie, c'est vraiment magnifique, n'est-ce pas?... Magnifique!* But, of course, in reality, that makes no sense at all. You can't get time to stop…. Time never stops…."

But for me, I thought, time had stopped since I had met Diane. I had been living in a never-changing present in which each moment was equally precious, and wasn't that what love, true love, always was?

Joan went on, *"Le temps ne s'arrête jamais, jamais . . .* never…. At least, for me, it certainly doesn't. I can't believe that I've been here a month—that month has gone by in a flash, an absolute flash, and next week I'll be with you in La Baule…."

She fixed her gaze on Diane, who lowered her eyes, took up her spoon, and nervously stirred her tea.

"…and ten days later, I'll be back in London. *C'est incroyable, vraiment."*

For me her revelation of Diane's departure was a positive unbelievable bolt from the blue. Did it really mean that Diane was leaving in a few days and leaving for good and that this was the end and that I would never see her again? I sat there stunned, waiting for some explanation, some correction from Diane, but none was immediately forthcoming.

There was an awkward silence. Joan looked at her watch.

"We'd better be off," she said, "or time will catch up with us. *O temps, suspends ton vol!"*

When we left the tearoom Joan and Gregory swept off ahead, and Diane and I followed some distance behind.

A deep chasm seemed to divide us as we strolled along. Finally Diane reached nervously across it to say that she was sorry that I had to learn of her departure from Joan. Her family was going to La Baule on the coast for the month of August and she had to go along, but she had already explained to her parents that she had to return early to prepare for an examination. She didn't really need the time to study, but she smiled as she gazed across at me, that would mean we would have more time together.

Diane's reassurance did little to calm my fear that her departure for the coast would bring an end to our relationship. That evening I lay awake for hours, jolted every few minutes by the slamming of the gate to the Jardin des Prébendes.

Walking to the Institut the next morning with Signorina Emilia, my mind wandered off and I made two terrible mistakes in French. They were the sort, the Signorina seemed to take pleasure in reminding me, that only a beginner would make. She was well aware that I knew better, and why on earth, she asked, did I not apply myself and show what I was really capable of. Her admonition proved fruitless and my *dictées* that morning were disastrous.

That evening I joined the Swedish contingent at the Univers, but was put off by their bright chatter and went early to bed. The next day was much the same, and then on the third day a letter came from Bourges, from Diane. She wrote:

> Darling,
>
> Our liaison is not at all like those banal, uninteresting adventures that we each know so well. It has about it something mysterious and profound. But perhaps I am mistaken and our difference of nationality is the cause of its strangeness. For the moment, darling, let us not think of the future but of the happy possibility of seeing each other again before the final cruel separation. I don't exist without you; the air I breathe is heavy and thick, and everything about me is dull and meaningless. This afternoon some friends came over. I danced a little but my heart was not in it, I couldn't stop thinking of our marvelous secret. Only Joan knows about it . . . At lunch today, it was

terrible. After a discussion of little
interest that I won't bore you with,
Mother said suddenly that it was a
shame that I didn't marry an
Englishman . . . or an American. Joan
couldn't stop smiling and I think that
Mother guessed what was going on. She
watches me constantly and that begins
to trouble me. I love you.

Diane.

Joan will bring you this letter when she
returns to Tours. That way, you will
have it more quickly.

Diane's words about our "marvelous secret" erased any
doubts that I had had. I carried the letter about with me for days,
folding and unfolding it, touching it, smelling it, reading it over
and over to myself. I took it with me a few days later when
Chester and I cycled to Loches; the thought of it brightened up
the gray, thick walls of this château, which had belonged for
centuries to the counts of Anjou and then to the Plantaganets of
England. It evoked much of the history of Touraine, and was a
fitting climax to all the visits we had made. It was here that Joan
of Arc had had her second meeting with the Dauphin and had
instructed him to proceed to Rheims, where he would be
crowned king of France.

Loches had once been a graceful palace but it had also
been a terrifying prison. Its sinister keep, completed about 1070,
once imprisoned Ludovico Sforza the Moor, the duke of Milan,
for eight years, who, legend has it, died blinded by the sun on the
day of his release. He had carved, in large letters, on the walls of
his cell: HE WHO IS NOT HAPPY.

A few days later I might have carved in large letters on
my wall: HE WHO *IS* HAPPY.

Another note came from Diane, saying how beautiful it was to be at the seaside but how desolate she felt to be without me and urging me to come to join her. That was followed shortly afterward by a postcard with a photograph showing the broad circle of the beach at La Baule with the words:

"Please write or come soon, Ever yours,"

I went.

VI

La Baule: Sea and Salt

To her glorious perfume that I carried always with me was already added the salt smell and taste of the sea. I was drunk for days just thinking about Diane waiting for me there where the waves would be rolling in. My mind wandered ever more than usual at the Institut, and Signorina Emilia reprimanded me for my slips in idiom.

"*A quoi pensez-vous?*" she would ask.

"*A rien,*" I would answer.

"*A rien?*" she would repeat, rolling the "r" in her determined way, and I would stare blankly ahead.

I said nothing to her or to the others at the pension about my plans for a seaside excursion. I didn't quite see how I would manage such a visit financially, but then I discovered that there were student rates on the trains and that through the Institut I could obtain a modest room somewhere in the area.

I asked Karl, the young Czech at the pension, if he would be willing to accompany me to La Baule and share the expense of a room and he agreed. Karl spoke French with extreme deliberation and there was a gentleness in his reserve. He seldom smiled but when he did, it seemed that his whole being would light up if only for a second or two. We had taken several bicycle trips together and I had grown quite fond of him. We reserved a room right on the sea, in the small village of Le Croisic just outside of La Baule.

The train was packed: every young person in central France appeared to be headed for the seashore that day. Whatever space in the third-class compartments that was not filled with bodies was taken up by luggage. Those who were not students vacationing were others taking advantage of their *congés payés*. The French Parliament had two years before passed a law granting all French employees fifteen days (two weeks) of paid vacation.

At the mention of this law at the table one day, Madame Biéron had remarked that now with the *congés payés* it would be impossible to go to any beach—every one of them would be covered with waste paper and rubbish. Most of these people, she said, had never been to the seashore in their lives and had not the faintest idea of how to behave when they got there.

Karl and I stood for almost the entire trip in the passageway with our heads out the window. While my body shook to the rumble of the train wheels—and their steady back-along, back-along, back-along—I breathed in the hot air with its mixture of sand and steam and in my mind went over and over the lines that kept returning to me:

> Oh, I remember swimming in the Cher,
> Light filtering down through the trees...

Karl looked at me and smiled. I had told him nothing about Diane but he understood that somehow, somewhere, and for some reason, I was, or that I soon would be, supremely happy.

From time to time as I gazed off into space, I caught the outlines of Signorina Emilia's stern disapproving face. When she guessed that I was going off for the weekend, she had immediately communicated her extreme displeasure. Such a journey would clearly take me away from my studies, and more than that, she intimated that I was clearly up to no good.

Our pension at Le Croisic was in a little stone building perched on a jumble of rocks with a small front terrace where we took our meals. As we sat the first evening enjoying a dinner of a thick steaming fish soup followed by a delicious, unidentifiable, but clearly fresh, fried fish, almost as if on schedule two Breton women strolled past. With their bobbing white headdresses, they looked as if they had caught pieces of the white clouds above them.

I went to bed that night with the pounding of the surf in my ears and the taste of salt on my tongue.

The next afternoon, at a spot on the beach at La Baule that Diane had carefully designated in a final letter, I found her where she said she would be.

Her skin had taken on a little color and the hair that brushed her cheek seemed streaked with silver. Her blue eyes in the bright sunlight now had under the scintillating dark lashes a mauve glint.

She was seated like a queen under a blue-striped beach umbrella, surrounded by a group of feminine attendants. As if to pay court, one of them would bend from time to time to whisper something in her ear, then turn and run laughing toward the waves. Diane appeared to be urging them on, rewarding each one with a bit of gossip or verbal refreshment of some sort.

I sat down on the sand nearby, but Diane acknowledged my presence only with a sly gaze in my direction. After a while, seemingly weary of the attention of her minions, she made her own way to the waves. I followed her.

She stood for a moment looking out toward the west while the breakers broke over her ankles. Then as she moved gradually forward, a larger wave broke over her breasts and she plunged into the water. I plunged in after her and as together we reached the top of an incoming wave, I began to attempt to speak to her.

"*Tu m'as manqué terriblement,*" I said, and just as the word *manqué* emerged from my mouth a great gush of salt water came in, an apparent attempt to fill the gap that I was trying to describe. My message of missing her was swallowed up at once by the sea.

"*Tu m'as manqué,*" desperately I tried again. And this time a giant wave slapped me square in the face and I went under.

It crossed my mind, as I came up, that with my hair slicked back on my head by the waves, I must indeed look like the seal that she had said was my totem animal. But if I was a seal, I was certainly not performing with a seal's agility in the water. I was splashing wildly about while Diane continued to glide blissfully by. With her hair carefully tucked under her bathing cap, I doubted that she had heard anything that I had said.

Back at the umbrella when she took off her bathing cap and let her gold hair come tumbling out, I thought that I would finally have a chance to get close to her but her companions again rushed up to surround her and keep me at a distance.

This routine was repeated several times in the course of the afternoon. The sun beat down on the gray-green breakers, and after each swim, Diane returned, calm and regal, to take her place under the umbrella, and I, awkward seal that I clearly was, flapped about at the edges.

Toward the end of the afternoon as her companions drifted off one after the other, we began to amble back under the pine trees to the cottage that her parents had rented for the summer.

Diane let me know at once that I would not be allowed to come near the house. Her parents did not know of my existence and her father would be furious if he found out.

We wandered slowly past the villas that had the odd gingerbread look of misplaced mountain chalets, all with peculiar and frequently pretentious names, "Mon Rêve," "Soupir d'Eté," "Le Paradis Trouvé," their windows laden with pots of geraniums and petunias. Diane appeared more and more determined to distance herself from me. If I asked a question, she would pretend not to hear or to gaze puzzled and dumfounded and then say something that had no connection whatever with what we had been discussing. My frustration grew with every step we took.

The Villa Salammbô, her parents' place, on the avenue Maréchal Joffre, was far less romantic than its name implied. A square, squat brick structure with a peaked roof, it sat back from the road in a little grove of pine trees behind a white picket fence.

The closer we came to it, Diane grew more and more nervous, fearful apparently that her father would at any moment emerge and find her in the company of this unexplained American. She hurriedly gave me a peck on the cheek and said that she would meet me as planned the next day in front of the Hôtel Royal. She closed the gate behind her and took a few steps to the front door.

Her abrupt leave-taking made me feel that everything had gone wrong and for no discernable reason. I had the odd sensation that she had left me holding something in my hands and when I gazed down at them, I could see that my hands held nothing but the darkness that thickened with every instant.

I stood there for some time transfixed, unsure of what to do or where to go. Then, of a sudden, as if I were stepping over the edge of reality, I pushed open the gate and moved cautiously in behind the shrubbery and the pine trees to a place only a few feet from the house from which I could gaze into the bright dining room where Diane and her family were sitting down to dinner.

They had gathered, father, mother, and two daughters, at a heavy square table lighted from above by an octagonal salmon pink-shaded lamp the fringe of which cast fishbone-fine shadows on the edges of the tablecloth. The lamp caught the profile of the father and mother seated at opposite ends of the table and shone full on Diane, seated directly opposite the window. I wondered, when she looked up and out, if she didn't see me standing there a few feet away, but her face showed no expression whatever. The faces of the father and mother were equally expressionless and the head of Diane's little sister nodded doll-like slightly from time to time. There was an air of solemnity about everything that made me hold my breath for fear that my heavy breathing would sweep through and like a sudden gust of wind break a glass or overturn and crack a plate. Framed by the window, the scene, centered around the still life of baguette, salad, fruit and wine, resembled an eighteenth-century genre painting, one entitled, I thought, "The Daughter's Return," with a stern father's disapproval indicated by the position of his knife and fork. It was the depiction of an enchanted house fixed out of time and space, from which the beautiful daughter could never escape. It was the center of what seemed a distant and alien world to which I knew that somehow I would never belong and which I would contemplate with unending amazement. How long I stood there I don't know but I carried the scene in my head on the bus back to Le Croisic until finally the waves pounding on the rocks cut through the fish-bone fine shadows on the edge of my bed and I dropped off to sleep.

Diane had told me that the next day she would have to accompany her mother on a shopping tour and would not be able to meet me until four in the afternoon.

Karl went off early on his own to examine the waterfront of the village and with the morning to myself, I began to explore the area between Le Croisic and La Baule. The French enjoy giving sentimental names to places and here they had gone all out to create what on a map looked for all the world like a giant valentine. The coast between Saint-Nazaire and Le Croisic was designated as La Côte d'Amour and at its center was the fine sandy beach of La Baule.

The beach, stretching for three miles between Pornichet and Le Pouliguen, one of the most beautiful in France, opened out, a giant fan of mother-of-pearl. At the east end a segment of pine trees planted to hold the sand of the dunes in check was called the Bois d'Amour. Love was clearly everywhere; this was a land meant for lovers.

The sea along the Côte d'Amour had carved out of the rocks breathtaking formations, the Polar Bear, the Devil's Bridge, tokens of love to which the pounding breakers offered up every second bouquets of iridescent spray.

I was gazing out on the green lawn of the Hôtel Royal toward the flower beds of the esplanade of the Casino when Diane appeared wearing a soft cotton blouse, a pleated skirt, and Grecian sandals (what the French call *spartiates*). She put down her little straw purse and began at once to tell me everything that she had been doing. She described in detail the visit to the market with her mother, the fresh fish, vegetables and fruit, as if she were presenting these on a platter then and there. She turned without pausing to an account of the recent visit of her English friend Joan, who was for me one of the most pretentious and least interesting students at the Institut. But Diane described in loving detail all the special, quirky English aspects of her character that in her eyes made for Joan's inimitable charm.

I waited in vain for any mention of our feelings for each other, I took her hand in mine and held it firmly against my chest.

"But tell me something about yourself," I said. "What have *you* been doing?"

She looked startled, and then gazing out toward the spot where we had been in the water together the day before, she said, "Me? . . . Why, nothing, nothing really."

She drew back her hand.

"Come," she said, as she stood up, "let me show you a little bit of La Baule."

Off we went down the embankment past a series of splendid hotels, one called, of course, the Splendid, and any number of ornate peaked structures, down the boulevard des Dunes onto the boulevard de l'Océan. There we turned left onto the avenue des Dryades, and the pine trees of the Bois d'Amour. We sat down on a bench at the edge of the Théâtre de Verdure.

Diane had said little during our walk and if her silence had disturbed me, here it appeared to be the most intimate form of conversation. It was the trees—or rather the dryads, the spirit of the trees—that spoke and seemed to say everything that we had in our hearts.

Back at the Royal, Diane laid her head, as we sat, gently on my shoulder and there it stayed for what seems, in retrospect, an eternity.

Then suddenly she got up and said, "My sister is waiting for me. I'll see you tomorrow morning," and off she went in the direction of the Villa Salammbô.

I sat for a few minutes then followed slowly in her direction. A short way down on the green lawn of the Hôtel Royal I came upon a little merry-go-round taking children on the rides of their lives. It was a tiny turn-of-the-century carousel, all swirling flowers, ribbons, and bows, caryatid-guarded golden coaches and a sequence of astounding animals. I caught sight of a little girl, her arms firmly around the neck of the giraffe she had mounted and right behind her a boy on a rooster about his size that seemed ready to carry him off through the air.

Parlez-moi d'amour, the carousel sang as it went around.

Diane and I met, as planned, the next morning at the bookshop adjacent to the Gare des Autocars in the place de la Victoire.

I arrived early and purchased a book, the beginning of which I knew very well, and the remainder of which I was eager to read. It was *Le Grand Meaulnes* (The Wanderer) by Alain-Fournier.

I had just put it down and had opened a tourist guide to La Baule that showed a field of violets, which the city had once cultivated. In the middle of the field stood a white-frocked young lady, who looked for all the world like Diane. As I raised my eyes, I met hers. There she was in front of me.

"What is the book you bought?" she asked. Without waiting for my answer, she gazed scornfully down at my acquisition.

"What a boring book," she said.

I was speechless, unprepared for such an announcement. How, I wondered, could she possibly find boring a book written about a place that she knew well because it was where she had grown up, and a book by Alain-Fournier, a local author, who had been widely acclaimed.

In my mind I went over the wonderful scene in which the tall schoolboy, *le grand Meaulnes*, loses his way while en route to meet someone at the railway station and wanders, as in a dream, into a country fête where he finds everyone inexplicably in costume.

All the characters who had risen so beautifully from the pages now moved before me as I sought to cope with Diane's dismissal.

"Boring?..." I asked. "That wonderful opening sequence that is like every student's dream. I felt that it was certainly mine."

"But not mine, I suppose," she said.

There was an awkward pause.

"I wanted to tell you—how can I put it so that it doesn't hurt you terribly? . . . I just wanted to say . . ."

She hesitated.

"I wanted to tell you that I think it would be better if we didn't see each other . . . if we didn't see each other . . . any more."

"Because of your father?" I asked. "Has he found out about me—about us? Even though he was indeed her father, he had no right to control her life and surely she was not going to let him put an end to what had been a dream, one like the dream I had loved so much in the book I had just bought.

She gazed again down at that book.

"No, it isn't my father . . . It's just *me*. I know how deeply you feel and I thought that I felt the same way but I see now that all this has been a passing attraction. For me I see now that it was just . . ."

She looked for the word.

". . . a *flirt*."

She used the English word that sounded strange indeed as the point and climax of her French sentence. It made her dismissal of me all the more cutting when it came as it did with a word she had lifted from my language. It was as if she had chosen to stab me with my own knife.

I had never before heard the word used this way in French. I knew it in English, of course, but for me "flirt" was usually a verb, not a noun.

She was using a woman's wiles to gain the admiration and affection of a man without any intention of responding to the

feelings that she had aroused in him. She was being a coquette—
a "flirt," if she wanted to use the word as a noun—and what she
had been practicing was "flirtation," pure and simple.

She had been frivolous, trifling, playing with me and
enjoying the play to the full.

That evening Karl and I sat facing each other at dinner
and again he could see that I didn't want to speak and he kindly
asked no questions. The silence after a while became a bit too
heavy and he tried, in his tentative French, to break it. He told
me about his day and his trip around Le Croisic. After dinner we
went for a walk into the village and then came back to sit for a
while on the rocks staring out at the sea. When he went up to
bed, I told him that I'd like to remain a while longer and just
enjoy the sound of the waves.

But I didn't remain long on the rocks. I made my way
slowly to the salt marshes behind Le Croisic. There numerous
acres form a great checkerboard of little salt pans in which the
sea salt is collected. The seawater is brought into the marshes
through canals and is trapped in tidal reservoirs that become
gradually shallower and shallower until the water is held in what
are called *oeillets*—eyelets—where it is only about two inches
deep. Here from June until September men—called *paludiers*—
with long wooden rakes collect the salt that has formed on the
bottom and rake it to dry in little platforms on the banks and then
pile it in larger heaps—*mulons*—on the edge of the salt pans
before carrying it off to be stored in sheds.

This desolate landscape seemed indeed the proper setting
for my state of absolute despair. The salt in the tears that filled
my eyes was reflected in the salted eyelets around me. The moon
was full that night and as I gazed out over the saltpans I had the
impression of walking on the moon's surface, so unreal was the
setting. I had seen photographs of the *paludiers* in their curious
costumes that they no longer wore—the shorts and felt vests, the
rims of their felt hats turned up at the edges like half moons.
Perhaps because of their unusual occupation they felt as I did at
the moment a curious affinity for the moon.

I began to review all the stages of my involvement with Diane, wondering how in the world I could have accepted all that she said as true devotion, when as she had put it bluntly, the whole affair was for her merely a "flirt." I kept returning in my mind to that word thrown out at me as if to rub salt in my wound and to make me suffer all the more by twisting in this manner the very language I spoke. As I walked along, I thought of all the letters in which I had poured out my heart to her, wishing now that I could erase every word.

The thought of those letters called up from the depth of consciousness a much earlier scene of rejection. I must have been seven or eight years old at the time, in the third grade, and in the classroom, as children so often do, we were passing notes back and forth, in this case love notes. I had apparently sent some passionate ones to several of the most attractive girls in the room. I evidently saw no reason why my love should be concentrated on any single girl. Why should love, if it meant what I thought it meant, be in any way limited. The teacher intercepted a good number of my notes, and before I realized what was happening, she had me stand before the class and read them out loud. Tears poured down my cheeks as I stood there, forced to reveal all my innermost feelings. It was the worst punishment that she could have inflicted. A fat ugly woman, she wore that day a black beaded dress, and, as I gazed at her, the black beads were little razor-sharp slivers that cut through my flesh. All that I had given of myself was cut to pieces and vilified. Now as I stared out at the salt eyelets that surrounded me, those slivers again cut through my consciousness, made even sharper by memory.

As I wandered on around the salt pans, the words of Ronsard came back to me as they often had that summer:

> Quand vous serez bien vieille, au soir, à la
> chandelle…

And I pictured Diane as she might be one day, bent over the fire like the old woman Ronsard had described, regretting her disdain for my love. It was perhaps some comfort to think that I was not the first young man to suffer from unrequited love. But how I wished I had been able to put forth my feelings in verses like those of Ronsard!

On the train the next day returning to Tours, the rumble of the wheels brought back over and over the lines I had composed that summer, not immortal ones like those of Ronsard, but all that I had now with which to console myself:

> Oh, I remember swimming in the Cher,
> Light filtering down through the trees…

And I understood now why I had completed that quatrain with the more somber lines, evoking another summer memory that now appeared much more to the point:

> The perilous passageway at Blois
> And the murder of Henri de Guise.

All the joy that the garden of France had brought me during those lovely months was now gone.

Back at the pension, I soon found that things were not at all the same. Signorina Emilia had departed suddenly for Milan, having received word that her mother was ill. I missed her company on the way to the Institut, her clipped speech, and the steady dry rattle of her admonitions, and thought of her alone somewhere with the heavy worn black leather bag and all its curled-up slips of paper bearing her innumerable surprising idioms.

Without the Signorina's urging me in and out of class to work harder, the daily routine became almost unbearable. The long sessions and the interminable lists of new idioms along with the painstaking translation into French of *Dr. Jekyll and Mr. Hyde* were remarkably tedious and unrewarding. If the classes at the Institut lost one of its Italian stars with the departure of Signorina Emilia, Italy's presence had decidedly increased. A dozen tall handsome young Italian men had arrived and like an occupying army had taken over the school. All dressed elegantly in stiffly pressed white slacks, white shirts, and white shoes, they moved together in military formation. Their French was hesitant but exact. Their responses in class came as if carefully rehearsed. Their presence cast a pall over everything, in the classroom as well as on the terrace where they gathered always in a group, talking only to one another and ignoring the others of us. It may have been their resemblance to oppressive, antiseptic, military hospital attendants that drove me to my bed—with a high fever and a very bad cold.

"Nothing to worry about," said Madame Biéron; she would take care of me and before long she did.

Marguerite arrived in my room carrying a tray of what looked like small jelly jars: they were *ventouses* or suction cups, which she proceeded to heat up by inserting a lighted piece of paper into each one. When the cup was hot, she clamped it on to my back. Before long she had affixed an entire circle of these cups where they began to work like angry mouths drawing out the bad blood from my lungs. Once the whole batch was installed, she pulled the cover up over me and left me, assuring me that I would soon feel very much better. With this glass carapace on my back, I felt transformed into some kind of armadillo being roasted on a spit. While I lay for what seemed an eternity with the glass mouths sucking at my back, my delirium was broken by the clanging of the gate in the Jardin, which rather than opening out onto the green lawn was in my mind leading straight into the steaming pits of Hell. When Marguerite returned to remove the cups, I certainly did feel better.

But no sooner had my fever abated and I paused to review my financial situation did I realize that I was running very short of money and that I might not have enough left to cover the rest of my stay. I stopped spending evenings at the Univers, and with other students who were having a similar problem, I found my way to the pawnshop, which I discovered in French had the rather bizarre name of *mont-de-piété*. To my mind the word should have been *pitié*, for resorting to it was indeed a shameful, pitiable transaction. The French slang for "pawn" ("to leave things with one's aunt"—*mettre des choses chez sa tante*) seemed to make the matter even more humiliating. The other slang expression "to put something *au clou*" (to have something locked up) seemed a far more exact description of what I was about to do.

I had little to pawn, but before I could get very far, Madame Biéron somehow realized, without my having said anything, that I was running out of cash and told me that if I wished I could send her the remainder of what I owed when I got back home.

Summer was drawing to a close: the days grew darker, each one emptier than the one before. All the joy that Charles Trenet had been singing about had evaporated.

As soon as we returned from La Baule, Karl left at once for Prague, prompted perhaps by Hitler's designs on Czechoslovakia. I hoped that he would not have to don the uniform that his ramrod stance seemed to call for even though it was totally alien to his nature.

The Institut arranged for a group of us to visit what remained of the priory that Charles IX had presented to Ronsard. It was here on the island of Saint-Cosme in the Loire near Tours that the poet had died and his remains had only recently been discovered, his skeleton bearing the marks of the crippling arthritis of his later years. During the French Revolution the priory had been sold off as a farm and the chapel where Ronsard was buried had become a barn, the roof of which had collapsed. In 1932 the society Sauvegarde de l'Art Français acquired the property and began its restoration.

The visit to this little island with its weeping willows and sandy shore that the poet loved should have brought on something of the joy of spring that he celebrated so magnificently. But it brought instead the cold chill of a winter wind that had pursued him most of his life. He had felt it first when as a sixteen-year-old page boy he had been a member of a diplomatic mission to Germany. He had returned, as the result of a serious ear infection, almost totally deaf.

It should have cheered me no end to stand there in the bright room with its great fireplace and its wooden beams where the Prince of Poets had lived and worked but I could think only of the cold December day when he died and of the horses' hooves later pounding his buried bones. I could think only of his tragic destiny to have to wait three centuries to be finally and widely acclaimed as he deserved to be.

My notebooks were filled with French idioms and I kept picking through them as through the remains of a great feast in preparation for the final examination. I felt completely unprepared and ready for disastrous results. I began to regret all the long nights of conversation with Diane which had eased my heart but by being limited a good part of the time to the same few words had not appreciably increased my vocabulary. On the day of reckoning I paid the price for my idle evenings. I felt miserable afterward as I gathered my books and prepared to depart.

The railroad station, in the buffet of which we had enjoyed so many delightful dinners, was filled the day we left. I was exchanging addresses with Gregory and making plans to join him on a quick visit to Versailles during our brief stop-over in Paris when into the station, along with her friend Joan, looking paler and more than ever like a wilted asparagus, came Diane, as fresh and lovely as she had been the night she walked into my life. She was wearing the same gray and gold sweater with her golden brown hair pulled up above it. She might have been Diane de Poitiers ready for a ride through the park of Chenonceaux.

She looked my way, nodded, and smiled. Although she was only a few feet away, it was a distant smile as if intended for someone she had just met. I went on discussing with Gregory our proposed side-trip to Versailles, the grandest of all the châteaux and a fitting one to end our summer in this country of châteaux.

A few minutes later when I presented my ticket to the

stationmaster, he informed me that I had forgotten to have it stamped by the Institut and therefore he could not give me the discount that was allowed. The train was due to arrive in a few minutes and there was nothing for me to do but return to the Institut, get the proper stamp and take the next train, which would mean, among other things, canceling the trip to Versailles.

When the train pulled in, I stood beside Diane saying farewell to Gregory and Joan, promising to meet them again some other summer but knowing deep down that it was highly unlikely that such a reunion would ever take place.

My mistake with my ticket was, I felt, the essence of my stupidity in Diane's eyes and in mine, my final humiliation. I nodded mechanically to her and set off as quickly as I could for the Institut without a glance back.

When I returned for the later train, there were very few students and no one that I knew. I boarded the train alone, leaving behind the garden of France and all its green-garlanded streams, wafted away now in the steam of the locomotive winding its way up toward Paris.

VII

The Return

The journey to Le Havre was sad and the arrival there was even sadder. I found that the boarding of the ship would not take place until evening and that I would have to spend the whole afternoon waiting in a café. I could not afford to order any food; I sat dejected over a cup of tea staring down the rough dark beach at the ship that would take me home. As I sat there, I reviewed every segment of my summer—all the evenings at the Univers with the circle of those faces from everywhere in Europe, the days in La Baule, and my bumbling departure from Tours. I longed for the gangplank to be pulled up and to have the Atlantic on every side of me again and to watch the shore of France slip off behind me.

Once on board I found myself seated this time at a table with Harrison Simmons, Professor of French at Ohio State University, and his wife Virginia, along with a very pretty young mulatto woman from Kansas City. She was, she told us, Vanessa Harmon, a dancer. Her stage name was Venice Harmonskaya, and she was returning from a successful tour of the European capitals, although she never made it clear which ones she had visited and what she had done there.

The occupants of this table, unlike those of the table I had shared on my way over, were not likely to join in reciting Ronsard's sonnet, "Quand vous serez bien vieille . . ." Professor Simmons seemed more intent on discussing the proportions of our cabins and the length of our voyage than on any recital of Renaissance poetry. Our ship, the *De Grasse*, he proudly informed us, had been named for the Admiral Count de Grasse who had distinguished himself in the Chesapeake Bay during the Revolutionary War on 5 September 1781, when he defeated the British and his victory had helped in their surrender to the Americans at Yorktown. On a ship named for so great a Naval officer, Professor Simmons assured us, we were certain to have an agreeable voyage.

"I certainly hope so," said Vanessa Harmon. "I'm terrified of getting sick if there is any stormy weather."

"No chance of that," said Professor Simmons. "We came back four years ago at this time and it was smooth sailing all the way."

After dinner that first evening, I paced the deck for several minutes, hoping that the salt air would clear my head of all the unfortunate images that remained of the summer, but when I returned to the upper bunk in my small cabin, I stared at the ceiling and the roll and pitch of the ship did little to soothe my nerves. I had the impression that for me all sensory perception had stopped. I was in an absolute void, unable to see, to smell, to touch anything around me. I dozed off finally in the empty terrifying darkness broken only by the incessant pounding of the ship's engines.

I came up the next morning and began to pace the deck again, attempting to roll back the darkness that still filled my head.

That darkness was broken suddenly by the voice of Vanessa Harmon.

"Good morning! *Bonjour*! *Bonjour*!" she called out as she sailed past on the tips of her toes, a golden cloud moving along as if there were nothing but joy in the world and nothing but the joy of wishing to share it.

I settled down in a deck chair and opened a copy of Baudelaire's *Les Fleurs du Mal*. I immediately felt that the poet was addressing me in the opening stanza of his first poem:

Hypocrite lecteur, mon semblable, mon frère.

I was indeed his hypocrite reader, his brother, ready to absorb whatever cynical messages he was ready to offer. I discovered at once his magnificent sonnet on the albatross, that bird that soars so beautifully in the air but moves so clumsily along when it alights on deck and becomes the butt of the sailors' jokes—the symbol of the poet exiled from his airy realm. I was about to move on to Baudelaire's other poetic visions when I looked up to find a young dark-haired woman who had slipped like a bird under the blanket on the deck chair at my side.

Birdlike she inquired: "What are you reading?"

I showed her.

"How wonderful," she said, shaking her feathery black bangs, "I adore his 'L'Invitation au Voyage,'" and began to recite the opening stanza:

> Mon enfant, ma soeur,
> Songe à la douceur
> D'aller là-bas vivre ensemble!
> Aimer à loisir,
> Aimer à mourir
> Au pays qui te resemble!...
>
> Là, tout n'est qu'ordre et beauté,
> Luxe, calme et volupté.

These lines have been beautifully rendered into English by Richard Wilbur:

> My child, my sister, dream
> How sweet all things would seem
> Were we in that kind land to live together,
> And there love slow and long,
> There love and die among
> Those scenes that image you, that sumptuous weather...
>
> There, there is nothing else but grace and measure,
> Richness, quietness, and pleasure.

Wilbur catches brilliantly the graceful movement of the stanza and even manages to render elegantly that seemingly untranslatable final phrase, "*luxe, calme, et volupté.*"

My new companion was Laure Martineau from Montreal and before long she was sharing Baudelaire's *luxe, calme, et volupté* quite explicitly with me. We were very soon in one deck chair wrapped in a single blanket with the book on the deck beside us. Laure was not only a charming and voluptuous companion she was also a splendid teacher who introduced me, a willing pupil, to several of the erotic positions outlined in the *Kama Sutra*, which we assumed with the greatest of ease under our blanket. How many days we spent thus, I can't remember but before we knew it we had to get up one afternoon to prepare ourselves for the *dîner d'adieu*. We passed a group of sailors and what they told us broke through the beautiful calm that we had been experiencing. News had just reached them that Prime Minister Chamberlain had returned to London after his meeting with Hitler in Munich. As he stepped off the plane, he assured the crowd greeting him that war with Germany had been avoided. The sailors on the *De Grasse* were not so sure. The umbrella that Chamberlain was always pictured with seemed to them not an emblem of triumph but rather one of defeat and submission.

The anger of the sailors turned against the British, who, as appeasers, had allowed Hitler to move ahead as he had and as they were certain he would continue to do.

"For us," one of them said, "that means that the German army will move into France and no Maginot Line will stop it."

We gazed out at the setting sun and the pompoms on the sailors' caps danced like poppies against the waves.

I announced the news to our table at the *dîner d'adieu* and the clink of the glasses that we lifted to toast each other in farewell had a hollow bell-like tone that cast a pall over the table.

We gathered in the smoking room afterwards for a Fête de Bienfaisance, one to benefit a seamen's charity. A handsome program printed especially for the occasion depicted a sad-eyed barefoot boy on the edge of a dock holding a baby in his arms, left desolate there we presumed, because of some misfortune at sea, not the happiest picture for us at the moment.

The passengers had volunteered that evening to display their talents. Jacqueline Elmore, a pianist, began with some quiet pieces by Chopin and Debussy. She was followed by Venice Harmonskaya dancing gracefully and solemnly to Rimsky-Korsakov's "Song of India." Walter Stone then tried to stir things up a bit by singing some of the songs of Charles Trenet that we had been hearing all summer: *"Y'a d'la joie"* and *"Je chante."* He concluded with the one about the silly customer from Toulouse who had left his horse by mistake with the hatcheck girl:

> Monsieur, Monsieur,
> Vous oubliez votre cheval.
> Ne laissez pas cet animal.
> Il y serait vraiment trop mal.

We all tried to join in the chorus and help that hatcheck girl get rid of the poor horse she had on her hands.

We gathered afterwards for a group photograph. Laure Martineau signed mine: *"En souvenir de notre voyage à bord du De Grasse. A mon petit ami, mon meilleur souvenir."*

We danced for the remainder of the evening, of which we all hoped to retain the "best memory."

That best memory was suddenly lost during the night: the *De Grasse* went through one of the worst storms it had encountered in years. The next morning I found very few people in the dining room, all clutching their chairs, looking pale and sick, as indeed most of them were. I started up to the deck to get some fresh air but almost got sick myself, having to step over others who lay moaning along the way. There is no sensation worse than that one has when the very deck on which one stands gives way at every moment, when every step is tentative and when the foot that is raised never seems to come down in the place for which it was intended. The walls move back and forth like the opening of an accordion and the wind, a cat of nine tails, lashes incessantly. And while the ears try to adjust to the drumbeat of the pounding waves, each one coming from farther and farther away, the ocean has become a many-headed monster constantly baring its huge white teeth while its tail lashes out in all directions. The worst part of all this is that the external upheaval moves at once to the interior, and the lashing, pounding, grinding never stops. When I returned to my cabin, my bunk seemed to break loose and to abandon me to the heavy sea. The storm grew more intense with every passing hour during the night until I felt that my eyeballs were breaking loose from their sockets and leaving me blind and empty-eyed in the howling cavern of darkness. This was the final night of our crossing and the ship rode out the storm but the calm that greeted us the final morning was anything but reassuring.

When I climbed up to the deck for the last time, stepping over any number of sick passengers along the way, I came on a sad gray scene: passengers were all lined up along the railing seeking a clear view of the skyline, which rather than coming forward to welcome them as they had expected it to, kept shifting and moving to and fro, the buildings like bobbins weaving in and out of the cotton fabric of the fog. The ship inched forward, the foghorn with positive deafening blasts marking every move. Where had they all come from, these somber faces at the railing, wet with fog and streaming with tears? I felt that I should somehow address those who had obviously reached this moment with great difficulty and were seeing New York for the first time and tell them that this gray curtain would lift when they disembarked and would reveal what all of us at the time called the "sunny side of the street."

When we finally reached the dock and the customs officials came aboard, they did little to dispel the melancholy nature of the scene. Some members of the Lincoln Brigade who had fought for the Spanish Republic were called forward and the officials snapped up their passports, which I understood would not be returned. What kind of country was this, I wondered, when citizens could be penalized for going abroad to fight for something they believed in.

When I went back down to fetch my suitcase, the waiter who had so efficiently looked after our table during the entire frequently unsteady crossing cornered me and bluntly informed me that the tip that I had left him was totally inadequate. I was well aware of this, I said, but unfortunately it was absolutely all that I had. I had kept just enough money for my trip home to St. Louis, with nothing whatever left over for food along the way. Indeed I had been hoarding apples, oranges, and bananas for days to help me through the long bus ride. When I thought of having given far too much to the steward who had helped with luggage on our arrival in Le Havre the irony made my humiliation at the moment all the greater.

I wanted to take refuge as soon as possible in the anonymity of the crowd. I lugged my heavy over-stuffed suitcase down the gangplank and hailed a taxi. At the bus station, just as I was preparing to lift my bag onto the bus, I saw Vanessa Harmon struggling with hers. She was accompanied by an elderly black woman, surely her grandmother. Together they proceeded slowly to seats in the back of the bus. I stood aside, covering my face when I climbed aboard myself, trying to prevent Vanessa from seeing me and having me witness the sad comedown that her arrival meant after her lovely time abroad.

When the bus pulled out of the station, leaving New York traffic behind for the flat stretch of the highway, my mind turned not to Baudelaire's *luxe, calme, et volupté*, which had characterized much of my return crossing, but rather to the line:

Hypocrite lecteur, mon semblable, mon frère . . .
This was truly I felt the voice of my brother, addressing me, his hypocrite reader, reminding him of the bitterness of his introduction to France, its literature, and its language.

VIII

Reprises: Fire and Ice

As soon as I got back, I plunged at once with great enthusiasm and determination into my work at the university. This was my last year and I wanted to make up for all the time that I had lost along the way. All summer I had felt ill-prepared alongside my European colleagues. They all knew so much more than I did. With a background in history, geography, and mythology, they could with the greatest ease call up any number of historical and literary references that left me completely in the cold. I wanted Europe, which I had barely touched, to open up for me as it clearly had for them. I began intensive work on languages, since it was language I thought that could open many doors and carry me far beyond my middle-American boundaries. In addition to a course in Old French, I took a survey course in Spanish literature, another in beginning Italian, along with other courses in Vulgar Latin and Shakespeare. The months went quickly by: my head was happily filled with great poetry in several languages and dramatic events of the European past that became for me as vivid as if they had happened yesterday.

My *certificat d'études françaises* at the Institut de Touraine arrived all beautifully laid out with signatures in a fine hand and notation of my embarrassing marks. An over-all "*Assez bien*" ("Rather good") and "*Bien*" ("Good") in Phonetics. Examining the certificate, I felt the presence of Signorina Emilia staring over my shoulder to remind me how much better these marks would have been had I really applied myself. But I began to put everything in perspective, and none of the moments of the summer, touring the châteaux, sitting and conversing with my fellow students at the Univers, swimming in the Cher, traveling to La Baule really seemed wasted, no matter how painful some of them now appeared.

Graduation came and went and I found that all my final efforts had not been in vain. I was asked to become an Assistant in the French Department for the following year and to teach two introductory classes while working for a Master's degree.

I had begun to view my attention to Diane with an ironic understanding, and guided by some unexplained impulse, one day I opened my French-English dictionary to the word *flirt*, and found the translation given as "flirtation, flirting" with these explanatory applications of the word: *"Avoir un flirt avec quelqu'un"* (To have a flirtation with someone) *"Ce n'est qu'un petit flirt entre eux"* (They are just having a fling), and *"Un de mes anciens flirts"* (An old flame of mine). So I thought that Diane and I had just been having a fling. I could see her now going over photographs of me that she had taken in La Baule and identifying me for a friend sitting beside her as "just an old flame of mine."

I began to feel that the decision in La Baule had definitely been imposed on her by her father, who was alarmed to think that she might have become involved with a young Englishman she had met the previous summer while in England or—even worse—with an American she had encountered this summer in Tours. I remembered that when I told Madame Biéron about my plans to travel to La Baule, she had explained that this popular resort was where upper-class parents took their daughters in July and August to find proper husbands for them. She laughed and said that I might well be selected as the perfect mate for somebody's daughter. But I realized now that she had feared that precisely the opposite would happen and that I would be quickly and brutally cast aside.

I had no sooner put this picture of brutal rejection out of my mind when it was replaced by a far more sinister one. On the first of September the news came that Hitler had invaded Poland, whose people had resisted valiantly but without any hope. On the third of September Great Britain and France declared war on Germany. What had happened to the peace that Chamberlain had so blithely announced? And where now were those French seamen with whom I had shared the news of Chamberlain's visit to Hitler? Where were they now and where would they be a year from now? And where, I wondered, were all my fellow students in Tours? I had already pictured Karl in uniform in Czechoslovakia, and the antiseptic masculine brigade that had arrived in immaculate white slacks was clearly made up of Italian Naval or Army intelligence personnel preparing themselves for Mussolini's invasion of southern France. And what of my dear friend Emilia Morandini? Was it really her mother who had called her home or was it the Fascist government for which she was forced to work and provide whatever information she could gather about the countryside of Touraine the—"garden of France"—the obvious destination of Mussolini's prospective invasion forces? My Swedish companions, of course, would be enrolled in their country's diplomatic service. Chester and I and the few other Americans would no doubt be the very last to be called up but I was absolutely certain that our time would also come.

And where—more importantly for me to know right now—was Diane? And how would this declaration of war affect her?

I did not have to wait long to know. The next week, almost exactly a year to the day after my return from Tours, a letter arrived from France, in the pale blue envelope that I knew so well and addressed in the fine hand that I so admired. Dated 24 August 1939, Villa Salammbô, avenue de la Gare, Pornichet (was this the same Villa Salammbô that I had known in La Baule or was it another with the same name at a different address?), it read:

Dear Bill,
      One year after our separation I have decided to send you this little note

which undoubtedly will have little affect on you. Do you remember, Bill, that you said once that one cannot forget; people are marked by their experiences and are in one way or another the reflection of their past. But I have a feeling that you no longer think so and that this young French student is now nothing but a distant vague episode of your stay abroad. But I have for some time felt that you were absolutely right. You have forgotten, I suppose, but I have not forgotten anything: the walk we took that day in La Baule, our conversation on the beach, our stroll under the pine trees, the book you bought the next morning in the bookstore, *Le Grand Meaulnes*, which I have now read and found that it did indeed have that dream quality that you had seen in it, and what else.

Each his turn. I no longer regret having made you suffer since now the thought of you fills me with such anguish. I've been wanting to tell you all this for some time but I couldn't bring myself to show my weakness before what amounts to your triumph. For that's what it is. But in spite of everything I wanted you to know all this before what is going to happen here very soon. We are all expecting war to come and I'm already arranging to take my place in the hospital where at least I'll be of some use. I have little hope, but if you wish to write, please do so at once to the address given above. On the bottom of your envelope put "Please Forward."

Will you want me, Bill, after all this? I certainly doubt it.

Diane

Would I want her? What a question! She was all that I had ever wanted, and she was now returning to me. Of course, I did remember everything very well and I did want her now more than ever—just when I thought that I might lose her and that I would be for her just "an old flame." I wrote back immediately sending a recent photograph and asking one of her in return. Her letter brought back in its pale blue paper all the color and the perfume of those violets that I had pictured that day in La Baule and evoked the vision of Diane in her white cotton dress and her Grecian sandals.

I had just begun to read *La Vita Nuova* of Dante and had memorized the famous sonnet:

> Tanto gentile e tanto honesta pare
> La donna mia quant'ella altrui salute…

I felt that my lovely Diane was that same gentle and honest lady and one who had also for me opened the door to a "new life."

She wrote back sending a photograph, one in which she was wearing the sweater that I loved so much, the one with the gray and black squares streaked with gold connecting thread and the gray ruffle at the neck. She was gazing out to one side and her hair fell at an angle across her forehead, just grazing one eyebrow.

I had moved into one of the dormitories of the university in order to be on hand for the two French classes I was teaching and to get on with my Master's thesis. Fascinated by the Middle Ages, I had chosen the field of Old French, the poetry of which in all its great variety from the *chansons de geste* to the ribald

110

folk songs was for me a delight to read and to decipher. The challenge of putting it into modern French and subsequently into English made me love the French language all the more. I had chosen to write on *Ami et Amile*, a thirteenth-century epic fragment, the tale of two knights bonded by an oath of friendship. Each one came to the support of the other in whatever crisis he faced. Their adventures related in what seemed to me magnificent poetry evoked a tapestry of the colorful life of the castles, villages, and countryside of the Middle Ages. Above my desk I now pinned the photograph of Diane and next to it one of Rodin's "The Kiss," that I had brought back from Paris.

Another letter arrived dated 10 January 1940, bearing the address of 20, rue San Francisco, Tours. It was accompanied by several photographs of Diane taken beside the partly frozen Loire. Of the chunks of ice floating in the river, she said, *"On dirait des nénuphars."* And indeed they did look exactly like giant waterlilies drifting past her. She explained that she had moved to Tours to continue her medical studies. She had decided not to become a dentist like her father but a full-fledged medical doctor.

"I will take care of our health, dear Bill, and you with your feeling for poetry will administer to our spiritual needs. All my comrades have left. There are only a few young people, mostly little girls. Life remains exactly as it was, and yet it has taken on a new aspect. It is the force of hope. The force is brutal and paradoxical but it exists in the heart of each of us and its purity allows us to move forward. Would it bore you to write me a long letter about your life, your friends, your studies? I would very much welcome that. Forgive me for giving so slight an affectionate tone to my letter, but that would surely be out of place and I don't have the courage to write what I think from day to day because I have such doubts about myself. But one thing I shall never doubt is that I esteem you more than anything in the world and that you can count on my deep and sincere friendship." She had signed this letter *"Une pauvre égarée."* And a poor lost soul she seemed to be as she poured out her heart to me. I tried in my next letter to recall our happy summer months and with it I sent an anthology of modern American poetry with notes on which poems I thought she should read.

Another letter from her soon followed:

> I remember the first time that you really entered my life. It was the first week of July and you were standing waiting for the parade to pass. Suddenly I loved you madly and it seemed to me that you were so much more distant, so much taller than all those other people gathered on the steps of the Hôtel de Ville. You were wearing a light gray suit, a white shirt with a necktie of deep red. This little detail may seem stupid but it shows how my mind concentrates on little things and overlooks much more important ones.
>
> Something tells me that with you I will be happy, with you I could live and breathe without suffering the anguish of insecurity and isolation. I no longer doubt your love, Bill. I know that you are worth more than anyone else in the world and I am sure that one day our destinies will be joined. When? Where? I don't now. I don't want to turn to our indecisive difficult future for it will probably be a long time before we see each other again. Unfortunately the tormented time through which we are passing may well last for years. Will you have the courage to wait?

I did have that courage I told myself as I read this over and over.

I wanted to share my joy at being in touch again with Diane but the few companions in whom I confided smiled with affectionate condescension as if I was slightly demented, which I may well have seemed to be, but a number of them did share my enthusiasm for the songs of Charles Trenet, and we met to listen to recordings of his joyous carefree and often silly lyrics. One of them appeared to be particularly apt:

Le monde entier fait 'Boum'

And the whole world was certainly going *boom*. All the moments of summer joy had sailed off like pink balloons while in this strange war—this *drôle de guerre*, as the French called it—nothing was happening although in the far distance there may have been the rumble of tanks. I would hunch over the radio but there was little news. The newspapers told us that Churchill declared that Britain was better prepared than it had been for World War I and there were long articles about the strength of the Maginot Line and positive statements from French generals about the readiness of the French army. That army sent the soldiers on the Maginot Line soccer balls to play with, and, in their idle moments, rosebushes to plant. Prime Minister Daladier announced that France would dismiss those soldiers who had two or more children. To get my mind off Diane I began to copy down in my journal some of the silly items that appeared to reflect the droll emptiness of the time. Dorothy Kilgallan in her column "Voice of Manhattan" wrote: "The newest dance fad in London is 'The Blackout'. It's done in the dark and features a change of partners . . . Ramon Novarro, the silent film star, who believes in reincarnation, followed a pet bird from the *Normandie* to a Broadway bird store and bought it—because aboard ship the bird had reminded him of his dead brother."

The wife of the head of the French Department at the university had a passion for the theater and to produce Molière's *Les Fourberies de Scapin* she collected a group of us with a wide range of accents and little histrionic ability, but somehow all of

Molière's inspired horse play took our minds off the unpleasantness of a war that seemed totally incomprehensible because it had been announced but was simply not taking place.

My room in the campus dormitory, although conveniently located not far from the front quadrangle with the library on the side and my office and classrooms on the other, was somber and depressing. Its wooden table and bookcases with their yellow-brown varnish reminded me of the olive-drab military uniforms that I had grown up with at Jefferson Barracks. I had thought that my work on the poetry of *Ami et Amile* would lift my spirit and triumph with bright panache over my dull surroundings and unhappy uneventful life. But rather than allowing me to concentrate on a poetic appreciation of the work, my advisor insisted on my preparing a chart of plot elements contrasting the different versions of the story—the Old French, the Anglo-Norman, and the Vulgar Latin. It all became about as inspiring as attempting to direct traffic in the heavy smog that was then engulfing St. Louis.

That winter was the coldest in St. Louis in a century and I thought frequently of those chunks of ice—those giant water lilies—floating past Diane in the photograph that she had sent me. There were mounds of snow everywhere and heavy black smoke enveloped the buildings. The streets became dark snow-flanked tunnels. When the sun did occasionally break through, it created stacks of filthy pockmarked slush. The St. Louis *Post-Dispatch* spoke of "Black Tuesday" when one of the heaviest smoke clouds settled down on the city like a suffocating blanket.

I would wake up at night in a cold sweat: in my nightmare I had been inching along on the ice through thick smoke, in my hands wringing out the rows of black headlines which exuded not water but blood. I would get up thinking of Diane over there somewhere making her rounds in a hospital— perhaps at the Château of Chenonceaux, if as in World War I it had now been taken over by the military.

No more letters came and I began to despair of ever hearing from her again. The winter had been one of total stagnation and the spring brought a sudden thaw, a terrifying gigantic muddy avalanche. All Europe broke apart and in my mind, with the German "blitzgrieg" its pieces came pouring down. On 10 May 1940 the Germans attacked and in three days the Netherlands had to surrender and Belgium had to give up half its territory. Before the end of the month the British Forces were forced to evacuate Dunkerque and the French were in full retreat. On 15 June Hitler attacked Paris and thousands of people fleeing the city were strafed by planes like herds of helpless cattle. Ten days later the French abandoned Tours, which had been its temporary seat of government, and the city was violently bombed for half an hour. France, totally crushed by the German military machine, appealed for peace from Bordeaux and on 22 June an armistice was signed at Rethondes in the forest of Campiègne in the same railroad car where Germans had surrendered on 11 November 1918. France was divided into an occupied zone, the North, the West, and the Southwest and a "zone *libre*" in the South administered by Maréchal Pétain.

Hitler's conquest had taken exactly five weeks. But not all of it had been so easy and in places its army had paid a heavy toll. When I heard that the cadets at the Academy of Saumur had fought valiantly and had held back the Germans from the Loire, I remembered watching them file past us in Tours on the Quatorze Juillet, 1938, their horses richly caparisoned and their sabers flashing.

In my mind's eye I could see Diane moving along among those wounded cadets remembering, as I did, how glorious they had once flashed by her on parade. Did she still remember, I wondered, that we had been standing side by side the day we'd watched them gloriously pass. I had finished my thesis and had received my Master's degree on the green lawn of the university. I had also received a fellowship to Princeton University to continue working for a doctorate but before I could think of accepting it, I had to clarify my position with the draft board and I soon found that Princeton would not support a deferment but would promise that the fellowship would be waiting after I had completed my military service. And what would that service be? Having grown up in the Army, I had seen too much of it and had no wish to answer its call. I decided to investigate the possibility of enlisting as my father had at my age, in the Navy. I soon discovered that I was eligible for the V-7 program of officer's training and could become a Naval Ensign after completing ninety days of concentrated work at Northwestern University in Chicago on the shores of Lake Michigan. I had all the qualifications necessary except for a background in mathematics. I would be admitted in the program only after I had completed a course in trigonometry. Since such a summer course was offered at the university, I immediately enrolled.

Having never been very strong in mathematics, I wondered how I would make out with trigonometry. To my amazement I found that I enjoyed it tremendously: it provided a kind of daily inner intellectual music that took my mind completely away from all that had been happening. For a month my mornings were spent in the classroom, my afternoons preparing for the next day and my evenings working as a waiter (a curb boy delivering trays of food to cars in a parking lot). All the same, despite all these activities I could not blot out that previous summer in Touraine. One Sunday afternoon images of it came flooding back and I set them down in this sonnet:

La Touraine

Through hushed, decaying surfaces, the swan,
classic, remote, and public in the park,
seals in silken shadow here at dawn
land once yours, once intimate as dark.
Now with naked ease past the duc de Guise,
past the Nazi hunting rabbits at Chambord,
it glides. Now candle-quaint, its clinical
whiteness clasps the puffed cheek of Ronsard.

Deliberate. Take back in crisp news-
paper pilfered articles of grief:
blood drips, trails crimson feather, feathers
        fuse —
thought, at best, is but a petty thief.
Bandage, the swan binds the black leaves,
        leaves—this
poem quite unlike one by Ronsard.

And, thinking of the Occupation and its consequences, I
put down this poem:

Au Tombeau du Maréchal Pet-de-Nain
            (*At the Tomb of Marshal Dwarf's-Fart*)

Travelers, pause—and lift your caps.
Bow your heads in the sun.
If your ears are good, you can hear perhaps
Taps at Carcassonne.

He mounted upon his milk-white steed
And led his people down the drain
With the Order of the Centipede
On a shield of cellophane.

His people cherished ancient roots
Their faith was sorely shaken:
He rode to the Spa and slicked his boots,
And had his picture taken.

His people asked him what to do.
He said: "Lay down your gun
And to the Centipede be true."
— He had stopped them at Verdun.

Travelers, pause—and lift your caps.
Bow your heads in the sun.
If your ears are good, you can hear perhaps
Taps at Carcassonne.

It is not clear to me now how exactly during that summer I met Delphine Dietrich. She was almost it seems an emanation of the place itself, of the dark winter and the smoky city that I had known. We probably met at one of the parties given on the edge of the university campus by some of the graduate students and young instructors. Her name and her presence were not unknown to me. She had been one of the conquests of Stuart Chambers and I recalled seeing her photograph in his archive of beautiful women. She had been a co-editor of the campus literary magazine and they had often examined student contributions while in bed together. Whatever beauty she once had had clearly faded: she was no longer the sylphlike figure that I remembered from the photograph. The weight that she had put on had brought with it a general neglect of her entire person so that everything about her seemed slightly askew, the hair falling in all directions at once and her blouses partially unbuttoned or clearly badly buttoned. It was as if her entire personality was held together by the deep throaty laugh that cut through the conversation with a certain authoritative abandon. The laugh had first attracted me and I was soon ready to follow wherever it led. And it soon took me to her house near the campus, a brick pile with a kind of Norman tower on one side. It was surrounded by massive flower beds and a broad green lawn that was being constantly nourished by sprinklers that made its cool green expanse particularly attractive in the torrid St. Louis summer.

Before long I was seated opposite her at a little table on the ground floor of that tower playing chess while we drank cold beer from pewter mugs. Her father had made a fortune in the shoe business and the house was furnished with huge dark chests, thick carpets, and heavy tables that were an opulent, if heavy-handed, declaration of authority and power. They exuded a kind of gemütlichkeit, so characteristic of the German side of St. Louis which I had until then avoided.

Shortly after we met I had taken Delphine for a drink at the apartment of one of my fellow instructors at the university but he had looked upon her with distinct disapproval and let me know soon afterwards that he found her "gross." So from then on we avoided my associates at the university and went out with friends of hers. Among them were her dentist Herman Gephardt and his wife Doris. Herman was a pink-faced jovial fellow and Doris was a bright flashy blonde, made all the brighter by the armory of gold ornaments with which she decked herself out. We would usually join them first in the basement family room of their house in South St. Louis where we had several beers before going to a nearby restaurant or a beer garden. At some of them we danced until the early morning hours usually to tunes like Johnny Mercer's "Jeepers Creepers":

> Jeepers Creepers
> Where'd you get those peepers?
> Jeepers Creepers!
> Where'd you get those eyes?
>
> Gosh all get up!
> How'd they get so lit up?
> Gosh all get up!
> How'd they get that size?

More often it was to the song that was sweeping the country and that we heard wherever we went. It was "Bei Mir Bist Du Schön" with lyrics by Jacob Jacobs and music by Sholom Secunda. It is worth quoting on its entirety since it caught so well the spirit of the time:

> "BEI MIR BIST DU SCHÖN" Please let me explain,
> "BEI MIR BIST DU SCHÖN" means that

you're grand, —
"BEI MIR BIST DU SCHÖN," —again   I'll
explain.
Boy: It means you're the fairest in the land, —
Girl: It means that my heart's at your command,
I could say, "Bella, Bella," even say "Voon-der-
bar,"—
Each language only helps me tell you how grand
you are,
I've tried to explain, —
"BEI MIR BIST DU SCHÖN," So, kiss me and
say you understand.

Kiss we did and after dancing, we would drive in the early morning hours, as a number of others did, to the Art Museum on a hill in Forest Park. There, in a well-known lovers lane beside the museum, we pulled up to make love in our car, and, I am embarrassed to say, depositing afterwards as others had, our used condoms on the branches of the trees outside the car windows. We drove off, leaving behind us in front of the Museum the statue of the man for whom the city was named. On horseback, the horse's left hoof raised, the statue depicted Saint Louis in a coat of mail, wearing a crown, sword held forth authoritatively in his right hand.

That whole summer I moved in a kind of haze. With Delphine Dietrich, whose initials I hadn't at first noticed were the same as those of Diane Davril, I was embracing the German side of the city that I had always deplored. Like Tours, my city was now occupied I felt when I read of the meetings of the South St. Louis German Bund that praised Hitler. Now when I opened the evening paper and every headline gave details of the latest German advance, I thought that a dark cloud like those that had covered St. Louis all winter had settled on it permanently. I struggled in a kind of suffocation through a world in which everything was out of focus, blurred and smudged over. I had decided now that it was unlikely that I would ever see Diane again, even though the clear outline of her face would from time to time break through the smoky haze.

The days, the nights, the months passed with a deadening sameness until finally on Sunday, 7 December, the world really did go *boom* with the Japanese attack on Pearl Harbor. It would be years, if ever, before the pieces of that world would be fitted together again in any sensible fashion.

Because I had had to abandon my teaching position at the university I took a temporary job typing manifests for a trucking company. In the corner of a little office on the St. Louis waterfront I sat for hours typing out lists of what was leaving St. Louis on the company's trucks.

In early January I also left for Chicago and my months of Naval training.

I hadn't seen Delphine Dietrich for several weeks, and when I arrived to say good-bye, she greeted me at the door by proudly pulling together the ends of a belt around her waist. She had been dieting, she said, and wanted me to see the result.

With the dark laugh that I knew so well, she led me to the little table where looking out at a blank snowy landscape, we sat for an hour drinking beer from pewter mugs.

I felt a deep sadness when I turned to leave her, but I did not look back. I never saw her again.

IX

Take Down This Book: the Translation

After four months of training in Chicago, I went in June 1942 as a Naval officer on my first assignment to Pearl Harbor. I worked there as a communications officer, but I was comfortably housed in what had been the Beach Walk Inn, around the corner from the luxurious Halekulani Hotel in Waikiki. (The Beach Walk Inn itself came pretty close to luxury.) This was far from being hardship duty, and indeed it may have been a feeling of guilt at having such an easy assignment while so many of my colleagues were off on dangerous operations that prompted me a month later to volunteer for duty on Palmyra, a coral atoll a thousand miles southwest of Honolulu (and oddly enough at that time still technically considered within its city limits) and just six degrees above the equator. The Navy had taken over this atoll a few years before from the Fullard-Leo family of Honolulu, who had owned it since 1922 and made it an important and indeed essential air base for planes on their way to the South Pacific.

Having been brought up on the edge of the Mississippi, I had never laid eyes on the ocean until I went to France in 1938 and I had never (with the exception of Manhattan) been on an island anywhere, and Palmyra was certainly not the kind of island that I had read, or thought, about. An atoll—the word is a Malay one—is a ring-like coral island and reef that nearly or entirely encloses a lagoon. This particular atoll consisted of only 680 acres, of approximately ten miles, of land emerging from the water. And this land, such as it is, had, of course, been built up by the living organism of coral which over the years had formed the reef and, having been built thus out of living things, it took on a special life of its own. The strips of land or coral outcroppings forming the ring were in places no wider than a small room and the landing strip for the planes in this case was indeed a strip. We were so completely surrounded by water at every minute wherever we walked or looked out that I had the impression of being like Huckleberry Finn on a raft—not on one floating down the Mississippi but on one let loose mid-ocean and caught by the reef in this lagoon.

The only vegetation consisted of a narrow line of palm trees and other tropical shrubbery perched along the coral outcropping that gave the whole the look of a feathered crown around the still, dazzling blue lagoon. The only inhabitants, other than the coconut crabs that fed on the coconuts they knocked down from the trees, were, nesting along the coral edges, hundreds of booby birds (the largest nesting colony of red-footed boobies in the world) whose awkward and clumsy look made it clear that their presence on land was only temporary. Once their large eggs had hatched, they would be off again into the air where, like the ugly albatross which they so resembled, they would in flight assume an absolutely majestic presence. Elsewhere the island air was adrift with flocks of small white and sooty terns unwound like a skein on the breeze that rose up from the sea and relieved the heat of the equatorial sun that beat down incessantly. Clouds would gather around the island's feathered rim and the light rain that fell for a few minutes almost every day formed a bead curtain that we thrust aside to gaze on a blue-green, rainbow-edged world constantly refreshed and reforming.

There was so much water in the air that in the wooden shacks we inhabited we had to have electric light bulbs burning constantly in the closets to protect our clothes and shoes from mildew. When we were not walking along the edge of the waves or parting the curtain of the rain, on our off hours, we went swimming, snorkeling in the lagoon, following the hordes of bright multicolored fish or gathering the speckled and spotted shells, some of which we strung together into necklaces to take back to the women who were waiting for us at home.

At every moment on this pristine, unspoiled, untouched bit of earth rising from the sea floor, I had the impression of being part of life beginning on the planet, life emerging from the water that covered so much of it. That impression was enhanced at night when I walked out, brushing aside the delicate terns that hovered in the air like the eyelashes on some giant eyeball, standing on the coral ring with the phosphorescent breakers pounding at my feet, the calm surface of the lagoon at my back and in the crystal-clear heavens the outline of the Southern Cross at my fingertips. I seemed at such moments to be not just at the edge of the earth but to be part of the earth's vision—a speck on earth's eyeball staring out into space. At such moments I felt a kinship with those Spanish mystic poets who walked out to gaze at the stars and found themselves not only at the center of the earth but at the very center of the universe, the work of some divine creator.

That contemplation did not perhaps take me, as it had the Spanish mystics, to the very center of the universe, but it certainly took me to the center of myself. Occupied as I had been for the past months with the war in the Pacific I had not thought of France nor of Diane for some time. But on one of the clearest most transparent of evenings when I walked out, brushing aside the murmuring flocks of terns hovering in mid-air, everything came back to me. Perhaps it was my touching, brushing aside the terns that recalled Diane's way at times with her hair. I sat down on the rocks on this tiny strip of land at the world's edge, the roaring waves depositing a circle of stars at my feet, and the whole summer came flooding back to me, first with the silly refrain:

> Oh, I remember swimming in the Cher,
> Light filtering down through the trees,
> The perilous passageway at Blois
> And the murder of Henri de Guise.

Then with the cool clear blue-green river-meadow and its garland of grasses, the Château of Chenonceaux stretching out over the water, the black and white tiles like the notes on a page of music, the winding stairway at Blois, so beautiful and yet so treacherous, the Jardin des Prébendes with the statue of laurel-wreathed Ronsard below my window, the banging of the iron gate that kept me awake, the dream of the girl I loved, and finally the words of Ronsard—"Quand vous serez bien vieille, au soir, à la chandelle" —that summed up the memory of my unrequited love.

But now rather than continuing in French, the poem shifted into English—to a poem of William Butler Yeats, based on Ronsard's, which I had recently discovered. I said it over now to myself:

> When you are old and gray and full of sleep,
> And nodding by the fire, take down this book,
> And slowly read, and dream of the soft look
> Your eyes had once, and of their shadows deep;
>
> How many loved your moments of glad grace,
> And loved your beauty with love false or true,
> But one man loved the pilgrim soul in you,
> And loved the sorrows of your changing face;
>
> And bending down beside the glowing bars,
> Murmur, a little sadly, how love fled
> And paced upon the mountains overhead
> And hid his face amid a crowd of stars.

Somehow Yeats had softened the words of Ronsard and made the memory of love, wrenching, cutting, and painful though it was, now more tolerable and more universal. All experience, I thought, awaits its symbolic translation in the psyche, and now with this literal translation I could finally put the whole experience to rest. I was indeed the one man who "had loved the pilgrim soul" in Diane and had loved "the sorrows of her changing face," and now in this dark and distant place on the world's edge, I put them aside, with all my youth and the force of a youthful love that I would never again experience.

~ ~ ~

It is late now and I have turned back one last time from the dark mirroring water of the East River. It has been refreshing to recall all this more than half a century later. And if I am able to put the story down, with all its flavor and its many complicated twists, in book form as I hope one day to do, will Diane perhaps take down the book and remember our time together in what I thought was the garden of the world? She would be my age now, old and gray, bending somewhere over a fire, perhaps on this cold winter evening.

I will be seventy-five next week just before I enter the New York Hospital for an operation to remove a small nodule on my right lung. Every moment now seems more precious than ever, especially those moments that memory brings back to me, as clear as those green-garlanded streams in Touraine.

"When you are old..." the words echo through my head and through this empty apartment. "We learn how to live when life is over," Montaigne has said, and I realize every day how little I have learned about being old. But oh, I do think that I know very well what it was like to be young.

Epilogue: A Proper Conclusion

I completed the first draft of this memoir shortly before my seventy-fifth birthday. I was scheduled at that time, as I have indicated, to enter the New York Hospital the following week for the removal of a small nodule on my right lung. But fortunately at the last moment my friend the eminent pulmonologist Dr. Marvin Sackner found that the hospital had misread the X-ray taken five years previously. The X-ray had shown that the nodule had not since changed its place or its size. Dr. Sackner believes the nodule that is still with me has in all likelihood been there since my childhood, the result of my having grown up in the limestone country of Missouri which I so admired and which, to my mind, the limestone landscape of Touraine in many ways resembles.

It has been fifteen years since I finished this account of my first journey to France and its immediate consequences. I put it aside but kept coming back to it, making small additions and corrections. Everything seemed to be there: I had told the whole truth but told it "slant," as Emily Dickinson said one should. "Success in circuit lies," she wrote. And in my circuitous recording of that summer of 1938, when I, along with those others in Tours, all so young and so full of life, were dancing with delight in what we thought was a garden but proved in reality to be the edge of a volcano soon to erupt, I had distilled, I thought, something of the bittersweet essence of an important period in my life and in that of the young woman I loved. But I realized in the end that I had not told the whole story. My love affair with France did not end with World War II. It continued for the rest of my life and a proper conclusion to this memoir had, however briefly, to take that into consideration.

William Butler Yeats said once that life is, in a sense, a preparation for something that never happens. He had been entirely prepared psychologically and imaginatively to marry the beautiful Maud Gonne, but she would not have him. It was of her that he thought in translating Ronsard's sonnet, "When you are old and gray and full of sleep," and it was her "pilgrim soul" that obsessed him completely and became for the rest of his life the imaginative focus of his existence. Similarly, everything in my life—my early concentration on the French language, my struggle to get to France, my awakening to the beauty of Touraine—all had provided an exact and thorough preparation for my marriage with Madeleine Dufay, whom I have presented in these pages as Diane Davril, and the vision of her is with me still.

I may have put aside in my mind my youthful love of Madeleine in 1942 there on Palmyra Island in the middle of the Pacific. But no sooner had I done so than my love affair with France, which she so clearly embodied, continued. I became personnel officer of the island air base and the yeoman who assisted me heard me speak of my study in France and of my graduate work in the Romance languages. He pointed out to me that Naval officers were advised to report regularly their efficiency in foreign languages and suggested that I write to inform the authorities in Washington, D.C., of my background and suggest that I be transferred to a place where I might be of greater service than I was on Palmyra. I did as he advised me and drafted a detailed letter that went off through the official channels. I never expected to hear anything back, but, to my great amazement in about two months I received orders transferring me from Palmyra to Casablanca, where the American Naval forces had recently landed. I flew up to Honolulu, shipped off to San Francisco, crossed the country by train, and then after some twenty days in the hold of a liberty ship, reached Oran in Algeria. From Oran, along with ten other naval officers, I went through the Atlas mountains by boxcar on those old narrow-gauge tracks. It was during Ramadan. The cars were filled with Moroccan and Algerian troops, who didn't eat during the day. So when the sun went down, the train had to stop in these little villages. A gun would be fired and the troops would get off, build fires along the track, and eat. The villagers would gather round and I'd interpret for my fellow Americans. Now when I hear about places like Sidi-bel-Abbès, the headquarters of the French Foreign Legion, I can remember very well how they looked at sundown.

I spent some three months in Casablanca as a communications officer, going up and down to Rabat and Port Lyautey every week as a courier. In January 1944 I replaced a British liaison officer on the aviso colonial, *La Grandière*. It had been built as a patrol vessel, or gunboat, for use in the French colonies. Three hundred fifty feet in length, it had three five-inch guns and a special apartment for a visiting governor. It was quite elegantly fitted out. I had far more pleasant quarters than I would have had on an American ship. *La Grandière* had fought against us in Casablanca. Afterwards, the ship had escorted convoys up and down the African coast between Dakar and Casablanca. Then the French Admiralty under the supervision of General De Gaulle asked that it be sent to join the American fleet in the South Pacific so as to be in touch with the French colonies there. I replaced the British officer since I was the only American officer around who spoke French.

We crossed the North Atlantic in January in terrible weather at a very dangerous time. It took us twenty-one days. We were one of the transports of a convoy of some thirty ships, and because we had little speed, we were towards the back. I was in charge of the ship's communications. I had a liaison party of three men—a radioman and two signalmen—and all the secret codes. The ship was refitted at the Norfolk Navy Yard and we sailed out through the Panama Canal to join the American South Pacific Fleet, stopping first at the Marquesas Islands and Tahiti.

Duty on *La Grandière* was far from perilous: on a number of occasions we pursued what proved to be nonexistent Japanese submarines but we never saw any real action. All the same, I had two very narrow escapes: the difference, in one instance, of a few hours, in the other, of a few seconds, and I would not have been here to tell my story. We had been tied up for several days next to an ammunition ship at Guadalcanal when suddenly and unexpectedly we received orders in the middle of the night to depart to escort a cargo ship. We sailed at dawn and a few hours later the ammunition ship blew up, and with it, the entire dock. Another time, in Espiritu Santo, the officers of an American training submarine, whom I had met ashore, invited me to accompany them on one of their regular runs. I was standing with the captain in the conning tower of the submarine when he spotted a plane from an incoming American carrier headed down on us. Within seconds he had the submarine, which the pilot had mistaken for a Japanese one, deep underwater. Although it shook like a battered cocktail shaker from the impact of the bombs, it managed to struggle back to port. This was my first, and only, venture on a submarine.

My last days on board the *La Grandière*, in 1945 when it had to return to France after the war had ended there, I devoted to completing a translation I had undertaken of Louis Aragon's *Les Yeux d'Elsa* and when I left the ship a number of these poems appeared in English in *Poetry* and other magazines. I was at the same time continuing to compose my own poems, and I spent many hours alone on deck reciting them to myself. These poems also found their way into the pages of *Poetry* and won an award. I decided that when I completed my service I would not accept the fellowship at Princeton and become a full-time professor of French but would continue graduate work in English and Comparative Literature. That study took me to Columbia University, and later, thanks to a Rhodes Scholarship, to Oxford. From then on for the next twenty years wherever I was — and much of the time I was Professor of English and Poet in Residence at Williams College in Massachusetts, Columbia University in New York, and Hollins College in Virginia — I went on writing my own poems but at the same time translating poems from French. I had started to read Jules Laforgue at the same time that I read T. S. Eliot, who was very much indebted to him, and I undertook the first extensive translation of Laforgue's work into English. In 1957 I published my *Selected Writings of Jules Laforgue*, which included in addition to selections of his poetry, segments of his correspondence and his art criticism. I later translated his *Moral Tales* (*Moralités légendaries*) and *Berlin: the City and the Court*. I also translated the poems of A. O. Barnabooth by Valery Larbaud under the title *Poems of a Multimillionaire* as well as the poems of other twentieth-century French poets. Here is my translation of "Pomegranates" by Paul Valéry:

> Pomegranates
>
> Pomegranates, fruit whose hard
> Rind to rioting seed must yield—
> One would think that he beheld
> The sundered forehead of a god!
>
> If the heat that you have borne,
> O pomegranates opened wide,
> Has with the irritant of pride,
> Made you crack your ruby walls,
>
> And if your desiccate, golden shell,
> From pressure of some hidden force,
> Breaks in brilliant gems of juice,
>
> I, at this luminous rupture, turn
> My dry thought inward and discern
> The architecture of the soul.

Ever since I completed it, I have kept a pomegranate perched beside me on my desk to remind me that what I am seeking in my work is to explore, as Valéry did, the "architecture of the soul."

The marriage that life had prepared me for did not take place as expected when I was young but it did when I was middle-aged and needed it more. I had been divorced for some years from Barbara Howes, my Bostonian poet-wife, and my small sons were usually with her for the Christmas holidays. I was happy to be invited by my friends, the poet Richard Wilbur and his wife Charlee, to come to Middletown, Connecticut, where he then taught at Wesleyan University, to spend this time with them and their family. But in 1965 I had heard nothing from them and presumed that for some reason the invitation for that year would not be forthcoming. I had made preliminary arrangements to join some other friends in the Bahamas and was just about to purchase the tickets when Charlee Wilbur telephoned.

"You must come for Christmas," she said. "A very beautiful French woman will be visiting the Viggianis and they are eager to have you meet her. We'll join the Viggianis in entertaining her and we want you to be with us. Please don't think of going anywhere else."

I accepted, of course, immediately. Charlee, I later learned, had never laid eyes on this great beauty, but I found that she had certainly been right to believe everything that she had heard about her. Carl Viggiani, the head of the French department, and his wife Janie had known Sonja Haussmann for many years. In 1949 a Canadian woman friend of Sonja's with whom she had stayed in London, Louisa Hemming, had met Janie Viggiani on shipboard and had told her that she looked so much like her French friend that they might have been sisters. The Viggianis went to call on Sonja and her husband, who then occupied a beautiful apartment in the Palais Royal. When Sonja opened the door on them, she saw what her friend Louisa had meant. She and Janie did indeed look much alike and good friends they became from that moment on. When Sonja divorced her husband and moved to a smaller apartment with her young son, she frequently entertained them and had put them up several times on their visits to Paris. The Viggianis had for many years invited her to come to visit them in Connecticut but she had never been able to manage it. She had made a long journey to visit cousins in Brazil, Peru, and Mexico and had stopped in New York on her return. Janie had come down to spend the night with her, but it was not until several years later when her son was to be off skiing that she thought that she could leave her job long enough to go to Connecticut. The Viggianis were delighted to know that she was coming. They immediately made plans for her to be part of several cocktail parties and dinners. Soon after she arrived they arranged to take her to have cocktails with the Wilburs. They explained that she was to meet a distinguished poet but said nothing about the fact that I would also be there: I was to be the big surprise.

Sonja had put on a beautiful brown lamb's wool sweater and skirt for the occasion, and was astonished when Janie asked her if she couldn't wear something a bit more flattering. When Janie explained that it was not a party but just a meeting with the poet and his wife and a friend of theirs, Sonja saw no reason to change. On that cold winter day that sweater and skirt and the simple but beautiful shoes that only Paris could produce made Sonja's slender graceful presence absolute perfection. Our meeting was quite simply a *coup de foudre*. Lightning struck us both and we knew immediately that we were made for each other. I don't remember a single thing that was said but just that Sonja, with a lovely resonant voice, spoke elegant English, informed and accentuated by a memorable laugh.

For the rest of the week we were constantly together and all the convivial gatherings were delightful from beginning to end but the only slightly disturbing aspect was the sense that we had of being carefully watched all the time. Everyone seemed to be wishing us well but at the same time wondering how things were really working out. I can understand their concern: we have since tried several times to bring people together and each time what looked like success proved to be utter failure. We couldn't wait to get away by ourselves. I asked Sonja if she would stay a bit longer in the country and drive with me to

Washington to attend Katherine Anne Porter's annual Twelfth Night dinner party. That would be wonderful, she said, thrilled by the prospect of meeting the author of *Ship of Fools*, which had just been published in Paris. So off we went in high spirits, stopping overnight in New York, where Seymour Lawrence, Katherine Anne Porter's publisher and mine, joined us.

The Twelfth Night Party, with the traditional burning of the Christmas greens in the fireplace, was a beautiful affair with an illustrious group of writers that included Robert Penn Warren and Eleanor Clark. Sonja was a great hit with everyone, as I knew she would be. Toward the end of the evening, Katherine Anne Porter took me aside and said: "If you don't marry that woman, you're a *fool*."

I replied that I had had marriage in mind from the moment that I first saw her.

Things then moved very quickly. Sonja came back to spend a week with me at Easter at Hollins College in Virginia, where I was Writer-in-Residence. I went to Paris the following summer, met her son Marc before he left for the island of Nordeney, near Hamburg in Germany, then went with her to Gassin above Cannes, where she'd planned to stay with an American lady friend. I rented a small house nearby so that my sons could get to know their future stepmother, and when they left in August to return to school, Sonja and I were married in Paris at the Mairie of the Sixth Arrondissement on 3 September, 1966. I flew back to New York, and Sonja followed in November. We have now been together for forty-two years.

Sonja Haussmann comes from an old Alsatian family and like many of those families that long ago made France the country of their choice, their allegiance and devotion to it was greater than that of many from the interior of the country who took being French for granted and did little to support it. When Sonja's father died in 1990, he was one of the few surviving pilots of World War I. He was forced to serve in the German army, having been a German citizen after the Franco-Prussian War, but in order not to have to fight against the French he became a pilot and served on the eastern front and his plane was brought down in Russia. After World War I, he established a security company in Strasbourg and had opened a branch of it in Paris before World War II. It eventually became the largest security company in France, an organization similar to Pinkerton, the Société Parisienne de Surveillance, which provided guards for buildings in Paris and armored cars for the transportation of gold and other valuables. Sonja was born and grew up in Strasbourg. Her parents had lost a small son at the age of four. When Sonja came along, her mother had expected the arrival of another son and had any number of boy's names ready. But as she was about to be taken in for delivery, her father asked what they should name the child if it proved to be a girl. Her mother, who had just heard a woman call out to her young daughter, "Sonia!", said, "Let's call her Sonia." And so Sonia she became and when she was a teen-ager and had started to reinvent herself, she decided that her name should be spelled with a "j" as it is in Sweden. She would thus be paying tribute to some of her Swedish forebears.

Shortly after we were married, my friend, the French writer Marc Chadourne with whom we stayed in the south of France, was much impressed by Sonja's beauty and elegance and referred to her as the "Swan of Strasbourg." And for me the Swan of Strasbourg she became and has remained ever since. She appears as such in my poem "The Tall Poets," a satirical piece about the New York poetic scene, which I completed as a Valentine for her in 1976, when the United States celebrated its bicentennial with great fanfare.

Sonja is also the subject of another poem dedicated to her, "Venice in the Fog," in which I wrote:

> Here seven years ago I walked at night through the fog, my steps echoing behind me.
>
> My past life rose up unmasked before me; and even then I could see your face—a face I had not yet seen—

Swim toward me—a bright fine-boned face parting
the spray before it, the figurehead of a ship . . .

And I gaze down now into the fog, and hear behind
me—echoing up through my life—

Your steps on the stair; you come in, cold from
your walk, and toss your purple cape on the
bed, its fur wet from the fog;

Your hair falls red about your throat; you turn from
the gold room and run the water in the bath,

Steam rising from it like fog, and below me
footsteps echo on the pavement; bell buoys
clang in the distance . . .

We have been together in many other cities throughout
the world—New York, Washington, London, Berlin, Rome,
Moscow, Budapest, Tokyo—but it is always to Paris, her
favorite city and mine, that we return, and where, now in our old
age, we hope to spend all the time we can.

Acknowledgments

This account of my 1938 summer of study in Tours centers around the French medical student I met there, Madeleine Dufay, whom I have called here Diane Davril. I chose the name "Diane" because when the war cut off our communication with each other in my memory she came more and more to embody the spirit of Touraine as represented by Diane de Poitiers. I often wondered how she had fared during the war, and when I returned to France in 1948, ten years later, I was tempted to try to find out. But in the end I decided to let her live on vividly in my memory, as she still does, and as I hope she will in these pages.

I have changed the names of several of my fellow students at the Institut de Touraine and of a number of students and professors at Washington University in St. Louis. Among the latter is my close associate, Clark Mills McBurney, whom I've called Stuart Chambers. I hope that my depiction of him in Paris as something of a dilettante womanizer will not detract unduly from my overall admiration for his work as a serious poet. He was my mentor, and, as a beginning writer, I was greatly indebted to him, as was my friend and colleague, Thomas Lanier Williams (later Tennessee Williams), on whom at the time he exerted a profoundly important influence.

This book would never have reached its final form without the valuable assistance of two friends. Barbara Ireson, the English writer and editor, who has lived for many years in Tours and knows Touraine and its history extremely well, has carefully reviewed every page, and Mary Bagg, the American editor and critic who has understood the intention and direction of my account has helped immensely in giving it its final shape. Other readers and friends who have offered valuable advice and suggestions are Elsie and Richard Racz, Kitty and John Drescher, Helen Handley Houghton, Ethelyn Atha Chase, Richard Wilbur, and Robert Bagg.

The painter Paul Rhoads, who has lived for many years near Chinon and who knows and loves the area, has done the drawings for the cover and for the chapter on the châteaux.

Most of the photographs I took myself in Tours, La Baule, and Le Croisic. For assistance in reprinting them I am grateful to Pivot Media, Florence, Massachusetts, and Nicholas Ireson in Tours. I am indebted to Christophe Tissot, the director of the Institut de Touraine, for permission to reproduce my early photograph of it.

The stanza from Richard Wilbur's translation of "L'invitation au voyage" by Charles Baudelaire, from his *New and Collected Poems*, published by Harcourt Brace Jovanovich, in 1988, copyright © 1988 by Richard Wilbur, is reprinted by permission of Richard Wilbur and Harcourt Brace Jovanovich. The paragraph from *Ronsard: Prince of Poets* by Morris Bishop, published in 1940, copyright © 1940 by Oxford University Press is reprinted by permission of University of Michigan Press. The translation of Ronsard's "When you are old and gray and full of sleep" is from *The Collected Poems of W. B. Yeats*, published by the Macmillan Company, London, 1950 is reprinted by permission of the Macmillan Company. I wish to thank Warner Brothers Music for permission to quote from the lyrics of the songs "Madame la Marquise" and "Bei Mir Bist Du Schön."

Several parts of *Dancing in the Garden* first appeared in other publications as follows: Chapter I, "Departure: the Great Dream," in *Per Contra: The International Journal of the Arts, Literature, and Ideas,* Summer 2008; Chapter VI, "La Baule: Sea and Salt," in the *Gettysburg Review*, Vol. 21, No. 4, Winter 2008; and "Epilogue: A Proper Conclusion," in a slightly different form, in *Veteran Recall: Americans in France Remember the War,* with a preface by Brigadier General James S. Dickey, by Hilary Kaiser, Editions Ileimdal, Bayeux, France, 1944, copyright © by Hilary Kaiser.

About the Author

William Jay Smith has been a major force in American letters for over half a century. He is the author of more than sixty books of poetry, children's verse, memoirs, and criticism. From 1968 to 1970 he served as Consultant in Poetry to the Library of Congress (a post now called the Poet Laureate). Two of his thirteen poetry collections were finalists for the National Book Award, and his translations have won awards from the French Academy, the Swedish Academy, and the Hungarian government.

Smith was born in Louisiana in 1918 and brought up at Jefferson Barracks, just south of St. Louis, Missouri. His memoir, *Army Brat* (1980), which recounts his unusual boyhood as the son of a professional soldier, a clarinetist in the Sixth Infantry Band, was widely acclaimed. Artur Lundkvist of the Swedish Academy said of it: "One would have to go back to the books of Kipling portraying military life seen through a child's eyes in order to find anything comparable."

Of Native American (Choctaw) descent, Smith explores his family roots in *The Cherokee Lottery* (2000), a poetic sequence describing the forced removal of Indian tribes east of the Mississippi. Harold Bloom has found the book to be Smith's "masterwork: taut, harrowing, eloquent, and profoundly memorable."

A member of the American Academy of Arts and Letters since 1975 and its former Vice President for Literature, he divides his time between Cummington, Massachusetts and Paris.